Routledge Library Editions

APPLIED DYNAMIC ECONOMICS

ECONOMICS

Routledge Library Editions – Economics

KEYNESIAN & POST-KEYNESIAN ECONOMICS
In 11 Volumes

I	Keynesian Economics	*Coddington*
II	Theories of the Bargaining Process	*Coddington*
III	The Social Science Imperialists	*Harcourt*
IV	On Political Economists and Modern Political Economy	*Sardoni*
V	Essays in the Theory of Economic Fluctuations	*Kalecki*
VI	Theory of Economic Dynamics	*Kalecki*
VII	Monetary Theory and Public Policy	*Kurihara*
VIII	Applied Dynamic Economics	*Kurihara*
IX	Post Keynesian Economics	*Kurihara*
X	Alternative Systems of Business Organization and of Workers' Remuneration	*Meade*
XI	Expectation, Enterprise and Profit	*Shackle*

APPLIED DYNAMIC ECONOMICS

KENNETH K KURIHARA

Routledge
Taylor & Francis Group
LONDON AND NEW YORK

First published in 1963

Reprinted in 2003 by
Routledge
2 Park Square, Milton Park, Abingdon, Oxon OX14 4RN
or
270 Madison Avenue, New York, NY 10016

First issued in paperback 2010

Routledge is an imprint of the Taylor & Francis Group

British Library Cataloguing in Publication Data
A CIP catalogue record for this book
is available from the British Library

Applied Dynamic Economics
ISBN 978-0-415-31375-9 (hbk)
ISBN 978-0-415-60785-8 (pbk)

Miniset: Keynesian & Post-Keynesian Economics

Series: Routledge Library Editions – Economics

APPLIED DYNAMIC ECONOMICS

Kenneth K. Kurihara
Professor of Economics, Rutgers University

London
GEORGE ALLEN & UNWIN LTD
RUSKIN HOUSE MUSEUM STREET

FIRST PUBLISHED IN 1963

TO SIR ROY HARROD

who is acknowledgedly more responsible than any others in our times for the birth and development of Dynamic Economics, pure and applied, and whose personal friendship towards me over the years I shall always treasure.

PREFACE

I have assembled here papers contributed to international journals on the common theme of *applied dynamic economics*. As the prefix 'applied' suggests, I am thinking of dynamic economics in such comprehensive terms as to encompass the philosophical, historical, technical and practical facets of the real world. Thus viewed, I believe dynamic economics acquires a new dimension that transcends the formal horizon.

Specific essays have been grouped together in three separate yet related parts, dealing respectively with 'Problems of Developed Economies', 'Problems of Developing Economies' and 'International Prosperity and Progress'. Reviews of relevant books by Sir Roy Harrod, Professor T. Haavelmo, Professor W. A. Lewis and Mr. T. Barna have been included as appendices. The reader may infer the range of this collection, not only from the multinational character of original publishers acknowledged (i.e. journals of England, India, Italy, Jamaica, Japan, Pakistan, Switzerland and the United States), but also from the titles of chapters and appendices. I hope this collection will be of some use in forwarding modern dynamic analysis and policy along the best tradition of classical 'Political Economy'.

For permission to reproduce my original contributions here I wish to thank the editors of *The Economic Journal*, *The American Economic Review*, *Econometrica*, *Kyklos*, *Economic Studies Quarterly*, *Social Research*, *Economia Internazionale*, *The American Journal of Economics and Sociology*, *The Indian Journal of Economics*, *The Indian Economic Journal*, *Social and Economic Studies*, *Kautilya*, *Panjab University Economist* and *Current History*.

Lastly I wish to record my thanks to Mrs E. Wenz of the Rutgers University Bureau of Economic Research for her excellent typing service.

KENNETH K. KURIHARA
Rutgers University

CONTENTS

PART I

PROBLEMS OF DEVELOPED ECONOMIES

CHAPTER 1

INFLATION IN THE POSTWAR AMERICAN ECONOMY*

We have had an inflationary boom of nearly eight years' standing since the end of World War II. Why did we not have the predicted depression and unemployment, as after World War I? How did the monetary policies of our Federal Reserve banks and the fiscal policies of our Treasury affect our postwar economy? What influence did the Korean War have on the development of general economic activity? What are the economic prospects for immediate years ahead? These are the questions this survey will attempt to answer—in the belief that 'we must study the present in the light of the past for the purpose of the future', to borrow from Lord Keynes.

I

Almost everybody expected a recession to accompany the end of World War II, for it was feared that there would no longer be that 'unlimited demand' which the war had created to absorb all that the economy could possibly produce with full employment. But the postwar boom continued almost uninterrupted, except for a dip in general prices in 1949 which looked for a while like the beginning of a recession. There are several factors which account for this continued inflationary boom, despite the contrary forecasts.

First, the uneasy peace that followed the end of global hostilities did not allow our defence expenditure to fall as drastically as was expected. No sooner did we hear the last shot fired than we heard new shots fired in Central and Southeast Asia, the Near and Middle East and elsewhere. Civil dissensions and international strife accompanied the end of World War II as they did the end of World War I, only more dramatically to launch that evasive kind of warfare known as 'cold war'. In those circumstances our defence expenditure could not be reduced below a record-high peace-time minimum.

Second, contrary to general expectations, reconversion difficulties were easily overcome so as to keep increasing civilian production—

* Originally appeared under the title of 'Inflation: The Outlook for the 1950's', *Current History*, May 1953.

more 'butter' along with more 'guns', as it were. This smooth return to peace production was doubtless facilitated by our general technical efficiency, the easing of priority allocations and the removal of price controls and the war-time excess profit tax. As a result, private accumulation of inventories and expansion of plant and equipment, which had been neglected during the war, proceeded faster than individuals and businesses were inclined to save out of current income. All this tended to expand our national income and employment. Lastly, the consuming public released its pent-up demand not only by spending more out of current income but by using part of its huge accumulated liquid assets in the form of savings accounts and cashable war-bonds. This last factor is what threw off many forecasters, both here in the United States and Great Britain.

These are the general reasons why the anticipated depression and mass unemployment did not occur in the immediate postwar period. But they are inadequate in explaining why the postwar inflationary boom has been *maintained* thus far. So we must turn to a consideration of more specific circumstances.

II

Whenever total demand exceeds total supply, general prices are inevitably bid up. This is the familiar story of price behaviour. When there is full employment of labour, that is, 'more jobs than men', as at present, the total supply of goods and services becomes virtually fixed. It is against the background of this inflexible full-employment output that we must evaluate the influence of our postwar monetary-fiscal measures designed primarily to cope with excessive demand. Now an 'inflationary gap' develops precisely because consumers, business and the Government want to spend on goods and services that are not there. Suppose, for example, that they want to spend $350 billion when the dollar value of available full-employment output is $300 billion at present prices. Then this excess of demand over supply is what causes an 'inflationary gap' equal in dollar value to that excess. Unless the gap so caused is wiped out somehow, it will be translated into higher general prices and so reduce the purchasing power of the dollar. This latter effect is what both consumers and the monetary authorities dread during a period of rising prices. To consumers, higher prices always mean that they get less goods and services with the same amount of money than before—a decrease in consumers' 'real income'. To the monetary authorities uncontrolled price hikes mean the debasement of money, in whose terms every economic activity is carried on, and the possible disruption of the functioning of our modern money economy.

Experience tells us that the monetary authorities are more effective in restraining a boom than in creating it. But our Federal Reserve policies may have been more effective in *sustaining* the postwar boom *without either a bust or a runaway inflation*—than is generally admitted. With a view to discouraging excessive credit expansion for possible spending sprees, the Federal Reserve authorities raised the legal reserve requirements of New York and Chicago member banks from 22 per cent to 26 per cent in September 1948. This action had the effect of tightening bank credit somewhat, since it meant that member banks had to have more cash as legal reserves to support and to justify the same amount of loans to customers. For reasons to be explained later in connection with fiscal policies, the higher reserve requirements did not prove to be a very effective anti-inflation weapon in practice. However, it must be added that the reduction of legal reserve requirements to 24 per cent in 1949 was entirely consistent with the recessionary tendency of that year.

In 1948, the Federal Reserve authorities raised the discount rate (interest rate at which they lend to member banks) slightly, thereby inducing member banks to raise their own rates on loans to customers. To the extent to which interest rates discouraged excessive borrowing and spending remains debatable, but it is probably not untrue to say that this 'tight money' policy served as a warning against the excessive desire to buy and sell on credit.

Another and novel experiment the Federal Reserve authorities introduced was consumer credit control known as 'Regulation W'. This measure was conceived and executed during the war and revived during the postwar period with a view to checking inflationary pressure as well as to minimizing the destabilizing influence of too rapid an accumulation of the stock of durables. Although the exact details of the law were revised from time to time to suit the requirements of general activity, 'Regulation W' had the effect of discouraging consumers from buying radios, television sets, automobiles and other specified durables on instalment credit. For it required merchants to raise the minimum down payments and to shorten the payment period, as far as instalment sales were concerned; it also required banks to scrutinize consumer loan applications very carefully. It is probably safe to say that in the absence of 'Regulation W' instalment buying would have increased the inflationary pressure considerably and that the post-Korean defence production was facilitated by the diversion of critical resources from the otherwise unrestricted production of consumer durables.

III

The impact of monetary policies on our postwar economy can be better understood in the context of our federal budget. Let us now reflect on the Treasury's fiscal operations.

In general, when the Treasury achieves a budgetary surplus, the effect on the economy as a whole is anti-inflationary; and when it incurs a budgetary deficit, the effect is inflationary. The latter is inflationary largely because the Government borrows and spends the newly created money by giving its IOU's (bonds) to the banking system. Government expenditure of the proceeds so obtained not only increases the income of the private sectors but also strengthens the liquidity positions and therefore lending propensities of commercial banks. Our government achieved a budgetary surplus during a brief period of 1947–48, but went into deficits coincidentally with the 1949 price dip and further on with the outbreak of the Korean War; it has been running on deficits ever since—at an annual rate of some $4 billion. It is obvious that the present deficit in the federal budget is due to the fact that defence requirements have increased total public expenditure in excess of tax and other public revenues. But let us trace back the fiscal policies to the immediate postwar period.

The personal income tax was *reduced* over the presidential veto in 1948, despite the then existing inflationary pressure. But this tax reduction was probably not a serious error of policy in the light of the 1949 decline of activity. However, it was considered an error of principle, since what was needed at that time was a tax *increase* unless expenditure was supposed to be reducible. For what modern fiscal theory stresses is budgetary flexibility with reference to the vicissitudes of general economic activity. It was not until after the outbreak of the Korean War that the income tax was increased both to pay for the war and to diminish the inflationary pressure accompanying emergency national mobilizations.

Another error of policy was seen in the Treasury's continued 'cheap money' policy which compelled the Federal Reserve banks to adhere to the war-time policy of supporting the stable government bond market. For under the 'support policy' the Federal Reserve banks were obliged to buy at par or better all the government securities that member banks chose to sell in order to acquire additional excess reserves for credit expansion, thereby nullifying the anti-inflationary effect of higher discount rates. However, the 'support policy' was modified when the Treasury decided to let rates (yields) on short-term government securities rise slightly in 1948. This

Treasury action made monetary policies operative again inasmuch as the discount rates had to be raised above the Treasury's short-term rates. Otherwise member banks could adjust their reserves for credit expansion by borrowing from the Reserve banks more cheaply than by selling government securities.

As mentioned before, higher interest rates consequent upon the Treasury's action probably had some restraining influence on excessive business borrowing and spending. But almost all economists agree that, while such a rise in short-term rates is justified during short-period inflation, higher long-term rates can have disastrous effects on such crucially important fields as housing and public utilities, not to mention the Government's long-range financing of welfare projects (e.g. education, public health, slum clearance, and so forth).

The above seems to be sufficient to indicate that fiscal policies, while they are potentially far more powerful a weapon than their monetary counterpart to fight inflation or deflation, are nevertheless subject to political distortions and complications. We have subsumed the impact of the Korean War in deficit spending, but its influence can be seen in the scare-buying of 1950 and in the expansion of plant and equipment to accommodate war orders in the subsequent years. However, the uncertainties surrounding the Korean War are of greater significance to the shape of things to come in general and to private business confidence in particular.

What are the prospects for the immediate future? There is wide agreement that the outlook for the immediate year or so is on the whole inflationary, albeit a trotting rather than galloping variety. This agreement is based on the assumption that nothing will meanwhile happen to reverse (1) full employment, (2) high business and consumer spending, (3) the Government's substantial deficit spending and (4) elastic bank credit. Expert opinions differ as to the crucial importance of any one particular factor, but they are unanimous as to the combined effect of all these factors. Let us extrapolate these factors forward to see what is likely to be in store for us.

That full employment sets a physical limit to output is a presumption in favour of continued inflationary pressure, provided that there is no severe limit to demand. But the very conditions of full employment generate such complications as would make it difficult to maintain full-employment booms. Not only are there no longer employable resources to increase total supply, but total demand tends to diminish because business spending becomes inhibited by the rising cost of production due to increased pressure on employed resources.

For this reason many businessmen are reportedly in favour of some unemployment 'to keep labour under control'. They see in aggressive organized labour an inroad upon their profit margins and so favour a regime of less than full employment as a matter of self-protection. They look dismally on the fact that organized labour has grown both numerically and in political strength during the past full-employment booms. The increasing practice of writing 'escalator clauses' into employment contracts, the postwar establishment of a Wage Stabilization Board, and the recent appointment of an AF of L man to a Cabinet post are but a few indicators of the growing importance of organized labour in the postwar United States. If, in other words, private business becomes convinced that full employment is injurious to its long-run interests, deflationary forces will be set in motion, whether in the form of active opposition to deficit spending or of 'capital on strike'.

At this point we may digress to discuss briefly a much subtler influence or attack on full employment which, if allowed to have free play, would doubtless reverse the present inflationary trend. I refer to that school of economic thought which is putting deflationary pressure on public policy, for both theoretical and practical reasons. Theoretically, this school is wedded to the notion that economic man's self-interest and market forces are always such as to make supply create its own demand, provided that there is no interference with the economic 'invisible hand'. It casts a carping doubt on the theoretical soundness of the Employment Act of 1946 which is designed to help 'maintain maximum production, employment, and purchasing power'. Practically, this school of thought is mainly concerned with maintaining maximum *laissez-faire* with a safe margin of unemployment on the ground that 'full employment at all costs' may destroy our democratic institutions, including free enterprise and free consumer choice.

For these reasons the above school of thought aims its criticisms at (1) monopolies which distort and endanger competitive market forces and (2) 'Keynesian' full-employment policies which justify the inflationary bias of the depression-weary generation. On the score of monopolies, organized labour is picked out as mainly responsible for 'wage-price spirals', although monopolized business is also criticized for passing higher costs on to higher consumer prices, instead of letting its profits after taxes absorb wage increases.

As to the second of these targets, Lord Keynes is supposed to be responsible for all kinds of irresponsible full-employment measures that threaten the traditional role of entrepreneurs as employers. It seems only fair to point out that Lord Keynes's famous book, *The*

General Theory of Employment, formalized what economic man intuitively felt and knew to be the right thing to do in free society, namely: to 'cure the disease (mass unemployment) whilst preserving efficiency and freedom'. The important qualification 'preserving efficiency and freedom' should dispel any misgivings about Keynesian policies necessarily leading to wild attempts to maintain 'full employment at all costs'. For all this, our problem today is not so much concerned with overcoming depression and mass unemployment (which was Keynes's problem) as with maintaining a full-employment boom once it has been attained—a new postwar problem that is vastly more difficult.

To get back to the main discussion, allusion was made earlier to the uncertainties surrounding the Korean War. This is because the armament programme, on which so much of present business outlays depends, is subject to sudden and perhaps drastic revision. In the press and especially business publications one cannot help discerning a sense of uneasiness about what some call 'war prosperity'. Sensible business leaders are seriously asking the question: 'Can we maintain prosperity without war orders?' If we, as a nation, cannot answer this question in the affirmative, we unwittingly justify the sinister propaganda charge that 'capitalist America cannot and will not have permanent prosperity without war'.

However that may be, business is becoming increasingly, and understandably, apprehensive about the consequences of over-accumulation of inventories and plant and equipment that is based on the precarious supposition that our present mobilization programme will expand rather than contract. Responsible business leaders are already emphasizing the need for prudence in the face of general uncertainties. Indicative of this business prudence is the fact that the excess of investment over business savings declined from an annual rate of $33 billion in 1951 to $13 billion in 1952. It is not very difficult to see that unless consumer spending and Government spending can be supposed to compensate for any drastic fall in business spending, deflation rather than more inflation will be the inevitable result.

What of consumer spending? At present consumers are spending at an annual rate of some $25 billion less than they are earning. This saving is, of course, a stabilizing factor so long as there is inflationary pressure. But it can cause trouble if a sharp cutback in military spending or in private investment occurs. Even on the most optimistic assumption, it seems doubtful that the consuming public will adjust its consumption-saving habits in such a way as to accommodate unpredictable changes in business or Government spending. The declining purchasing power of the consumer's dollar seems to be making its impact felt, notably in the case of expenditures on clothing that make up about 13 per cent of the average family budget. For since toward the end of 1951 clothing expenditures have been steadily going down. It is by no means certain that other consumer expenditures will not follow suit. There are some counterbalancing forces, though, such as fairly large liquid assets (e.g. savings accounts) in the hands of consumers, continuing farm-subsidies to keep up farm-income, and organized resistance to wage-cuts, to mention only a few. These tend to put some kind of a floor below which consumer demand may not fall.

As for the outlook on Government spending, the new Administration is presumably going to put an end to the 'era of spendthrift' and bring back the good old era of 'sound finance'. Be that as it may, whether or not we shall achieve a balanced budget, let alone a budgetary surplus, on a continuing basis crucially depends on something which is not entirely within our control, namely: the course of international events, including the progress and outcome of the Korean War. It remains to be seen whether the new Administration will be able to diverge very far downward from the Federal deficit of $14 billion estimated for 1952–53 by the previous Administration. If the present international tension is lessened to warrant a large reduction in military outlays, the Government will probably cease to be a major inflationary factor in the national economy. If, however, the pressure increases to make the Government spend more to supplement any deficiency of private investment that demobilizations may occasion, the Federal budget will most likely remain unbalanced to exert an inflationary influence. There may be some ground for the fear that the new Administration will go too far in the direction of disinflation, for its avowed 'economy in Government' can conceivably become a god to be worshipped, regardless of the overall requirements of particular periods of economic fluctuation.

There is no such fear as far as Federal Reserve authorities are concerned, for they are confidently expected to subordinate their monetary policies to the changing needs of the national economy as a whole instead of to any dogma. It seems fairly safe to hope that the monetary factor will not be allowed to play an aggravating role in the inflationary or deflationary trends ahead. Unfortunately it is difficult to entertain a similar hope with respect to fiscal policies, subject as they are to considerations other than their own merits.

While the immediate outlook is on the buoyant side, we cannot afford to be complacent about continuous full-employment booms being left to so fortuitous a thing as 'cold war' or the economic 'invisible hand'. Yet it would be amiss to go to the other extreme and to maintain that we are in for a catastrophic depression after Korea. The sounder attitude to take seems to be one of recognizing the latent deflationary forces below the inflationary surface and of meeting such forces as they try to raise their ugly head. For too much preoccupation with maintaining *laissez-faire* under inflationary full employment is just as self-defeating in the long run as too much pre-occupation with maintaining full employment regardless of ruinous inflationary consequences. Inflation may be today's main enemy, but deflation can be tomorrow's main enemy. This is the lesson of history.

CHAPTER 2

PROFESSOR HANSEN ON AMERICA'S ECONOMIC REVOLUTION*

On the eve of his retirement from Harvard University, Professor Alvin H. Hansen took stock of his turbulent teaching career, what he had taught and advocated, the interwar and postwar changes in economic thinking and policies, and above all the impact of 'the Keynesian Revolution' on the American economy. The result is his latest book, *The American Economy.*[1] There Professor Hansen equates America's economic revolution with the Keynesian Revolution and, more specifically, with a new combination of a *mixed economy* and a *welfare state*, and then professes a new faith in the possibility of secular exhilaration, instead of repeating the famous 'stagnation thesis'. The purpose of this essay is not to review Professor Hansen's book in any conventional manner but to discuss in some detail fundamental questions of public policy and economic theory which it raises but which he does not himself discuss, namely: (1) limitations on a mixed economy, and (2) limitations on a welfare state—in sum, qualitative and quantitative limitations on the development of the American economy along the lines envisaged by Professor Hansen.

To indicate such limitations is not to imply any basic disagreement with the *principle* of a welfare-oriented, mixed public-private economy but to suggest a need for improving its *technique* by reference, not to stifling dicta, but to changing data. One may sympathize with Professor Hansen's propensity to give greater emphasis to the optimistic aspects of the American economic revolution, and still feel that qualifying observations, such as will be made in this essay, might be of use to the American economy trying to achieve and maintain stable growth, and, by repercussion, to other mixed economies to which America's stable growth is a matter of common interest and concern.[2]

* Originally published under the same title in *Economic Journal*, September 1958.

[1] McGraw-Hill, New York, 1957.

[2] For a great international concern in the stability and growth of the American economy see *The Business Cycle in the Post-War World*, E. Lundberg, ed. (London: Macmillan, 1955), especially contributions by E. A. G. Robinson, S. Tsuru, J. J. Polak and N. Kaldor.

HANSEN ON AMERICA'S ECONOMIC REVOLUTION

I. LIMITATIONS ON A MIXED ECONOMY

Professor Hansen thinks of a mixed economy as one 'in which the powerful fiscal and monetary operations of an alert and informed government are playing a stabilizing and sustaining role'.[1] He recalls the gradual acceptance in America of Keynesian criticisms of *laissez-faire*, the gold standard, sound finance and other familiar earmarks of individualistic capitalism, leading up to the 1946 Employment Act, the President's Council of Economic Advisers, the Congressional Joint Economic Committee and the more public-spirited Federal Reserve System as *faits accompli.* Thus the Keynesian foundations of the American mixed economy are made unmistakably clear, though the relation of Keynesian economics and the welfare state is left less clear.

The above developments in the American economy are viewed as the practical manifestations of the Keynesian Revolution, whereby it is theoretically demonstrated that the parametric role of market prices fails to equate aggregate demand and supply, to bring about autonomatic full employment or even to ensure the optimal allocation of resources—for the economy as a whole. The question naturally arises as to whether the American economy undergoing the Keynesian Revolution, as such, has become as depression-proof and stagnation-proof as Professor Hansen *now* seems to believe.[2] To ask such a question is to imply that there may be more difficulties in the way of the successful completion of the Keynesian Revolution than Professor Hansen is willing to admit. Before discussing some of those difficulties, however, let us look at the specific reasons why Professor Hansen supposes the American economy to be 'on the march' toward stable growth and secular exhilaration.

Professor Hansen attributes his new faith and American people's new confidence in the possibility of stable growth to three structural changes in the American economy, which represent also three major characteristics of the American economic revolution: (1) the counter-cyclical and compensatory fiscal-monetary responsibilities of government as a permanent feature of public policy; (2) the commitment of the Federal Government to a policy of guiding the private sector to maintain 'maximum production, employment and purchasing power' in accordance with the Employment Act; and (3) such 'built-in-stabilizers' as the democratic welfare state is capable of providing on an increasing scale (e.g. progressive taxes, social security, farm-support programmes, public housing and mass education). Professor

[1] Hansen, *op. cit.*, p. 34.
[2] Compare his *Full Recovery or Stagnation?* (1938).

Hansen seems to consider these to be not only necessary conditions but also sufficient conditions for the stable growth of the American economy. The sufficiency of these conditions, however, may be questioned for a number of reasons.

We may discuss the first two conditions, leaving the third to the next section. Fiscal policies based on Keynesian theory are of the two broad types, one of which is designed to strengthen the propensity to consume and the other to stimulate the inducement to invest. These types of fiscal operations are not necessarily compatible with each other, however. Suppose that we follow the multiplier theory and let public-works expenditures act as a multiplicand. To be sure, consumption respending will increase effective demand, which will in turn induce some private investment, according to the familiar multiplier-acceleration interaction. But apart from the usual objections to the acceleration principle (the possible presence of excess capacity and the possible expectation of short-lived demand), there are two ways in which a permanent programme of public works may undermine the private propensity to invest. First, in so far as public-works expenditures are geared to productive projects, the productive capacity of the economy may increase relatively to its effective demand, only to depress the profitability of further investment, as Mr Harrod and Professor Domar have shown.[1] Second, once public-works programmes have been accepted as a matter of principle, it will be difficult not to concede the theoretical possibility of the Government providing all the necessary employment opportunities and all the necessary goods and services on a non-profit basis. Such a concession amounts to a tacit rejection of the supposed necessity of private enterprise for maximum employment and production. Thus a permanent programme of public works, however countercyclical, carries with it an implied threat to private investment and private enterprise, at least in the minds of entrepreneurs.[2]

Such adverse reactions on private investment and private enterprise are not, of course, arguments against the principle of public-works programmes, for private investment and private enterprise can have the same capacity-increasing, investment-depressing effect, but cannot have the stability of the whole economy as their primary objective, anyway. These adverse reactions are pointed out here by

[1] See R. F. Harrod, *Towards a Dynamic Economics* (1948), and E. D. Domar, *Essays in the Theory of Economic Growth* (1957). However, they call attention to the capacity-increasing effect of mainly *private* investment.

[2] Cf. S. S. Alexander, 'Opposition to Deficit Spending for the Prevention of Unemployment', *Income, Employment and Public Policy* (In Honour of A. H. Hansen), 1948. Professor Hansen, however, lightly dismisses such opposition as 'rapidly vanishing' (Hansen, *op. cit.*, p. 169).

way of qualifying the purely quantitative and one-sided analysis of public-works programmes as an income-employment generator. It would be a mistake, however, to draw the rash conclusion that public-works programmes are never compatible with private enterprise. Such a conclusion is as extreme as the opposite conclusion that public-works programmes are the quickest way to achieve state socialism. Professor Hansen, while he judiciously avoids such extreme conclusions, nevertheless overlooks the aforementioned antinomy of public expenditure programmes that discourages the private inducement to invest while at the same time encouraging greater induced consumption by the private sector receiving those public outlays as factor incomes.

Keynes was aware of the possibility that 'the Government programme may, through its effect on "confidence", . . . retard other investment'.[1] This awareness of the possible conflict between the aim of increasing induced consumption and the other aim of stimulating private investment led Keynes to mention 'pyramid-building, earthquakes, even wars'[2] as being better than *laissez-faire*. He did not, of course, favour such obviously wasteful public-expenditure projects, but the fact remains that those projects of the non-stock raising type, however wasteful, are in the nature of the case less competitive to private investment and private enterprise. Here lies the danger, despite Keynes's intentions to the contrary, that the desire not to impair business confidence may make policy-makers look upon 'pyramid-building' and 'wars' as the most practical form of compensatory expenditures. Thus perverted, Keynesian policies are naturally open to the criticism that they foster unproductive and undemocratic 'make-work' ventures, such as are historically associated with the Nazi regime in prewar Germany. Even though one can properly dismiss such a line of criticism as a gross misunderstanding of Keynes's intentions, one may not cavalierly disregard the above danger as an objective possibility. For this danger is a painful reminder of the antinomic character of Keynes's theory of effective demand, that is, a contradiction between the equally valid principles of inducing consumption and 'pump-priming' private investment, and hence an implied contradiction between public-expenditure programmes to increase the former and those to stimulate the latter.

Similarly, tax programmes to encourage private consumption will be found to come in frequent conflict with tax programmes to stimulate private investment. Progressive taxation, which Professor

[1] *General Theory*, p. 120.
[2] *Ibid.*, p. 129.

Hansen favours on both compensatory and welfare grounds, could be carried to a point where the private motive to accumulation, the profit motive to production and the private inducement to invest are all so reduced as to offset its beneficial effect on consumption-demand.[1] Such a possibility is especially strong in a full-employment economy, since progressive tax rates, tax subsidies to low-income families, a reduction in retrogressive sales-taxes and other tax measures to sustain consumption-demand in conditions of full employment would bid away fully employed resources from the capital-goods industries—at least in a relatively short period during which technological advance and population growth could not be relied upon to make up for the diminished quantity of capital. A tax measure to stimulate investment could also prove self-defeating, as Professor Hansen has himself hinted. The accelerated-depreciation tax policy, for example, could be pushed to a point where private firms are encouraged to 'scrap useful and comparatively new plant and equipment', which Professor Hansen criticizes as 'a highly wasteful use of resources',[2] but which one may criticize also as leading to such an over-accumulation of plant and equipment as to diminish the profitability of future investment. If investment-demand is thus reduced, income and induced consumption will fall via the reverse operation of the multiplier principle and in a self-defeating manner.

What of countercyclical monetary policy? If a cheap-money policy is taken as an integral part of Keynes's social philosophy as well as his economic theory, then far-reaching difficulties are bound to arise. On the one hand, Keynes's fundamental attitude toward the 'functionless investor' (rentier) would logically lead to an 'interest-free society', which Mr Harrod recommends and defends on the ground that 'it would enable us to dispense with the collectivist method of attacking capitalism'.[3] But the trouble may arise when, not the collectivist, but the entrepreneur for whose benefit an interest-free regime is intended, starts asking whether the Keynesian denial of interest as a defensible property income will not eventually cast a serious doubt on the propriety of profit as a property income and the institution of private ownership itself. Professor H. C. Wallich, perhaps sensing such entrepreneurial apprehensions, has already raised questions of this kind.[4] Both the traditional criticism of monopoly profits as violating

[1] Compare E. C. Brown, 'Business-Income Taxation and Investment Incentives', *Income, Employment and Public Policy*.

[2] Hansen, *op. cit.*, pp. 134–5.

[3] Harrod, *op. cit.*, p. 147.

[4] See his 'The Changing Significance of the Interest Rate', *American Economic Review*, December 1946.

the rules of the competitive game (because it represents the exploitation of an inelastic demand curve) and the trade union argument against profit-takers' tendency to make up for higher labour costs (due to higher-wage movements) by raising prices even when they can absorb them in reduced profits are indicative of profit being less functional than Keynes supposed on the tacit assumption of a competitive model. Thus viewed, the Keynesian cheap-money policy carries with it the far-reaching implication that the very entrepreneur whom it is intended to protect against the rentier's 'oppressive power . . . to exploit the scarcity-value of capital'[1] may himself face that 'euthanasia' which Keynes thought applicable only to 'the rentier aspect of capitalism'.

Professor Hansen does not discuss these fundamental questions of monetary policy, limiting himself to 'the dangers of large changes in interest rates'[2] to capital markets. He objects to drastic changes in interest rates on the ground that such interest changes, even when designed to promote price stability, cannot be brought about except at the risk of provoking 'general all-round instability of capital values' (presumably via the inverse relation of interest rates and capital values). Since this latter destabilizing effect on capital market ties the hands of the monetary authority, Professor Hansen makes that effect out to be a 'basic' case against monetary policy for fiscal policy. He comes close to admitting that if the monetary authority did not have to worry about possible capital losses to banks and insurance companies, a consequentially feasible dear-money policy might be effective in checking inflation. Such an admission would, of course, weaken his case for fiscal policy. Professor Hansen might have made a more cogent case for fiscal measures to reduce inflationary pressures, had he argued that the interest-inelasticity of public and private investment would render any excessive reliance on the rate policy largely unfruitful, and if he had frankly recognized the fact that the large and growing public debt of the United States sets a practical limit to the upward movement of interest rates. Even the interest elasticity of public-utility and housing enterprises (usually considered exceptions to the interest-inelasticity of investment in general) is likely to be reduced in the conditions in which the population is growing at a fairly rapid rate and the backlog of pent-up demand still lingering on—in sum, the postwar boom conditions tending to increase the marginal efficiency of capital relatively to any practical maximum rate of interest.

Professor Hansen could have shown that a short-run dear-money

[1] *General Theory*, p. 376.

[2] Hansen, *op. cit.*, pp. 53 ff.

policy to offset a reduction in the real value of interest income (though usually effected in the name of general anti-inflation policy) due to rising prices would run counter to the long-run objective of stimulating 'growth investment' in fixed capital to that Keynesian extent of 'the products of capital selling at a price proportioned to the labour, etc., embodied in them on just the same principles as govern the prices of consumption-goods into which capital-charges enter in an insignificant degree'.[1] In Professor Hansen's hands all the objections to interest-rate policies become largely an argument in favour of fiscal policy, instead of becoming also a basis for showing how difficult it is for the monetary authority to reconcile the rentier aspect of capitalism with its entrepreneurial aspect, a difficulty which even Keynes apparently underestimated. For Keynes apparently considered it both desirable and feasible to do away with the rentier aspect of capitalism without thereby seriously contradicting his fond purpose of encouraging the entrepreneur *et hoc genus omne*. Such a contradiction does not arise as long as one deals with the rate of interest relative to the marginal efficiency of capital, abstracting from dynamic shift factors affecting the marginal efficiency of capital *schedule* itself. But as soon as it is realized that the phenomenon of interest considered as a functionless reward has ominous implications for the phenomenon of profit and for the whole institution of private ownership, investment incentives may be reduced so as to shift the marginal efficiency of capital schedule downward, thus offsetting any beneficial effect which a low interest rate may have on planned investment.

So much for the limitations on a mixed economy, limitations arising not only from the antinomic nature of Keynes's own underconsumption-underinvestment theory but from the dualistic nature of a mixed public-private economy itself. Let us now turn to the other major American development in the economic field.

II. LIMITATIONS ON A WELFARE STATE

Professor Hansen conceives a welfare state primarily as 'a redistributor of income and a colossal purchaser of the products of private enterprise' and justifies it as 'a solid foundation upon which to build a full-employment programme'.[2] He makes allusion to Keynes as a *de facto* social-welfare reformer when he observes: 'The *General Theory*, with its emphasis on the consumption function, taught us, however, that the social-security programme was not only good

[1] *General Theory*, p. 221.
[2] Hansen, *op. cit.*, p. 38.

social ethics but also good economics.'[1] Thus Professor Hansen relates the American welfare state to Keynes through the latter's interest in an equitable distribution of income and wealth, the stabilization of employment and the promotion of consumption-demand. In other words, Keynes is thought of as having provided an *economic* justification of what had been largely a humanitarian sentiment, even though the idea of a welfare state antedates Keynes. The welfare state based on Keynesian economics, together with the mixed economy discussed in the preceding section, is supposed to guarantee the stable growth of the American economy. There are a number of serious limitations on the welfare state as a stabilizing and sustaining factor, however.

There is a strong possibility that welfare expenditures will seriously conflict with military expenditures in a nation that is more defence-conscious than it is welfare-conscious. Professor Hansen himself alludes to such a possibility when he says that 'the national-security budgets compete with the growing urgent need for much larger long-range social-welfare budgets' but that 'we should all agree that national security comes first'.[2] However, Professor Hansen gives us no satisfactory escape from the warfare-welfare dilemma, except to urge that America should 'increase *now* by a substantial amount our long-range public-welfare budgets' presumably without reducing 'our military programme'.[3] It is hard to see how the kind of long-range social welfare programme envisaged by Professor Hansen can be financed on an increasing and continuing basis without at the same time reducing defence expenditures even in so wealthy a country as the United States—unless the national income can be supposed to increase at a much faster rate than at present. Unlike an abstract welfare state that occupies a celestial space untroubled by so mundane a problem as the welfare *vs.* warfare controversy, a concrete welfare state must find shelter in a real world fraught with contending ideologies and conflicting scales of value. Until and unless the practical men of affairs become demonstrably willing and able to vote for larger welfare budgets than for defence budgets, they will, it is to be feared, continue to think of national welfare primarily in terms of military preparedness and so to frustrate such a genuinely welfare programme as Professor Hansen recommends on both economic and humanitarian grounds. The resulting welfare programme may fall far short of providing effective built-in stabilizers. This limitation is a limitation not so much on a welfare state

[1] *Ibid.*, p. 159 n.
[2] Hansen, *op. cit.*, p. 148.
[3] *Ibid.*, pp. 148–9.

per se as on a mixed welfare-warfare economy. In so far, moreover, as the welfare state has anything to do with Keynesian thinking, the above limitation is that of Keynes's and Professor Hansen's over-idealized notion of the state both as a superb balancing agent and as a supreme judge of social priorities.

Next, let us consider Professor Hansen's argument in favour of 'redistributive processes of the welfare state designed to broaden and deepen the consumption base'.[1] Once a fiscal redistribution of income and wealth has been accepted as conducive to economic stability and welfare, the next logical step will be to question not only the traditional theory of distribution but also the existing system of distribution based on private property and factor pricing. For it is natural for egalitarians to dispense with redistribution, fiscal or otherwise, if they feel that they can permanently solve the problem of income disparities by modifying property relations that predetermine those disparities. Thus, on the one side, the welfare state tends to encourage egalitarians of the 'underconsumption' type to move from a redistribution policy based on given property relations to a distribution system based on entirely different property relations and so to discourage private enterprise in general and private investment in particular. Keynes was himself somewhat responsible for this tendency, for he accepted J. A. Hobson's underconsumption doctrine tracing underemployment to inequality as being 'undoubtedly in the right',[2] albeit in conditions of *laissez-faire* investment.

On the other side, Keynes's economic theory built around the strategic importance of private investment, coupled with his social philosophy granting 'significant inequalities of incomes and wealth' as a useful concession to human motivation and as a helpful incentive to creative activities,[3] would serve to restrain any extreme egalitarian tendency which his other theory of underconsumption may foster. Realization of Keynes's antinomic attitude toward the question of distribution would probably have the ultimate effect of stopping the redistribution function of the welfare state short of the point where it could, via the otherwise increased quantitative importance of consumer incomes and expenditures, contribute substantially to the stabilization programme. Thus it is by no means obvious that the redistribution feature of the welfare state can be counted upon as providing so solid a basis for the full-employment programme as Professor Hansen claims.

Lastly, no discussion of the welfare state is complete without some

[1] Hansen, *op. cit.*, p. 157.

[2] *General Theory*, pp. 324–5.

[3] *General Theory*, p. 374.

reference to the possible effects of monopoly on consumer welfare, investment stability and technical progress. In so far as a welfare state represents also a strong anti-monopoly atmosphere, as it does in the United States, the notion of built-in stability becomes extremely ambiguous and incongruous. Perhaps this is the reason why Professor Hansen leaves out anti-monopoly legislation from his list of built-in stabilizers which the welfare state is supposed to provide. However, his professed predilection for a 'high-wage, low-profit' regime[1] is strongly suggestive of anti-monopoly volition. Professor M. Bronfenbrenner in a Schumpeterian critique has challenged Professor Hansen's 'high-wage, low-profit' scheme as of dubious compatibility with dynamic capitalism.[2] At any rate, it is important to consider the problem of monopoly in relation to the welfare state, both because monopoly has a vital bearing on the equitable distribution of income, and because monopoly is variously viewed as helping stable growth and as hindering it. Anti-monopoly legislation considered as an integral part of the welfare state will be found to present a serious dilemma for the American economy.

On the one hand, the reduction of monopoly may stimulate the private inducement to invest as well as the private propensity to consume via the sequence of lower consumer prices relative to money wages, higher real wage income, increased consumption expenditure, exhausted capacity in the consumer-goods industries, increased orders for capital goods and finally increased output of capital goods in the capital-goods industries. This beneficial effect of anti-monopoly legislation on consumer welfare and investment-demand is what Mrs Joan Robinson's explanation of monopolization implies.[3] Applied to the American economy, Mrs Robinson's implicit case against monopoly acquires cogency and plausibility, for in that economy the growth of monopoly has tended to strengthen the propensity to save (out of corporate profits) more than it has stimulated the inducement to invest. *Apropos*, Keynes warned against excessive corporate saving such as monopoly would encourage when he observed: 'It is possible . . . that the extreme financial conservatism of corporate finance in the United States, even during the slump, may account for it (the low marginal propensity to consume and hence a high leakage coefficient in the multiplier equation).'[4]

On the other hand, the same reduction of monopoly may militate

[1] See his *Economic Policy and Full Employment* (New York, 1947), pp. 48–9.

[2] See his 'Some Neglected Implications of Secular Inflation', in *Post-Keynesian Economics*.

[3] See her *The Accumulation of Capital* (London: Macmillan, 1956), p. 78.

[4] *General Theory*, p. 182.

against private investment if Schumpeter's theory of monopoly is correct. For according to Schumpeter, 'trustified capitalism' tends to promote innovational investment through: (*a*) a favourable reaction on the cost-reducing type of research and know-how; (*b*) the stimulating effect on innovations of stable monopoly profits due to the downward rigidity of monopoly prices; and (*c*) the encouraging effect of monopolized finance on the industrial application of available inventions and innovations.[1] The logical implication is that anti-monopoly legislation does the private inducement to invest more harm than good. However, Schumpeter's explicit case for monopoly as the 'creative destroyer' of dynamic capitalism and his implicit case against anti-monopoly legislation as a possible impinger on innovational investment are open to the following objections. First, monopoly may, via its decreasing effect on real wages (this via raising consumer prices relatively to money wages), depress consumption-demand and so offset any stimulating effect it may have on investment-demand. Second, monopoly may have the effect of making the adoption of capital-saving techniques (or labour-using ones) profitable via its decreasing effect on real wages, thus making for a weaker accelerator. Thirdly, monopoly may, via its tendency to restrict output, make the presence of excess capacity a normal phenomenon and so render the acceleration principle less operative than otherwise.

The main point to be stressed here is that the diametrically opposed views of monopoly as a force making for secular growth and as a force making for secular stagnation, in so far as they are taken to be both valid, would probably entail some compromise between extremely pro-monopolistic and extremely anti-monopolistic policies. The resulting half-hearted anti-monopoly programme of the welfare state can hardly be said to provide effective built-in stabilizers or to promote an equitable distribution of income and wealth. This last limitation is fundamentally a limitation on a mixed monopoly-competition economy. It is also a limitation of Keynes's theory (in contradistinction to post-Keynesian economics) lacking a macro-economic treatment of monopoly.

CONCLUDING OBSERVATIONS

Professor Hansen takes great pains to identify Keynesian policies with capitalism and to dissociate them from socialism. Thus after comparing Keynes's *General Theory* favourably with Marx's *Das Kapital*, Professor Hansen hastens to add: 'The book is not an attack

[1] See his *Capitalism, Socialism and Democracy* (1947), Chapter 8.

on private enterprise. Indeed Keynesian policies have . . . immeasurably strengthened the private enterprise system.'[1] By contrast, Keynes seemed willing to err on the side of socialism rather than on the side of capitalism. Thus the author of the *General Theory* proclaimed his sympathy with Gesell's book, the purpose of which 'as a whole may be described as the establishment of an anti-Marxian Socialism'.[2] True, it was a socialism of the anti-Marxian variety that Keynes also intended to establish theoretically, but it is significant that he did not say 'an anti-Marxian capitalism' instead. Perhaps this difference between Keynes and Professor Hansen is a reflection on their respective 'anti-capitalist volition' and 'pro-capitalist volition', as Schumpeter would say, but it may be a reflection also on two different political climates in which 'socialism' is a more or less discussable subject. Be that as it may, the fact that Professor Hansen finds it necessary to stress Keynes as a saviour of capitalism and to defend Keynesian policies against those criticizing them as 'socialistic' is strongly indicative of the underlying antinomy of Keynesian analysis and policies. For we have seen that Keynes's theory of consumption tends to encourage radical policies, while his theory of investment tends to encourage conservative policies. Our analysis of those antinomic elements would suggest that the mixed-economy, welfare-state scheme of things is likely to prove less solid a basis for stable growth than Professor Hansen supposes and less automatic a transition to a full democratic socialism than some followers of Keynes seem to imagine.[3]

Professor Hansen might be right in stressing the fiscal, monetary and other Keynesian policies designed to stabilize aggregate demand as adequate for the American economy with abundant resources but without stable markets. But such policies may not be adequate for

[1] Hansen, *The American Economy*, p. 167.

[2] *General Theory*, p. 355. See, in this regard, Mrs Joan Robinson's rather independent appraisal of Marx in her 'Marx and Keynes', *Collected Economic Papers* (1951).

[3] See, e.g. J. Strachey, *Contemporary Capitalism* (London: Victor Gollancz, 1956; H. Gaitskell, *Recent Developments in British Socialist Thinking* (London: Co-operative Union, 1956); C. A. R. Crosland, *The Future of Socialism* (London: Jonathan Cape, 1956). These writers may not consider themselves as followers of Keynes, but what they write seems to be in line with Keynesian thinking. In this regard, Professor P. T. Homan reports 'a thoughtful British socialist' as saying: 'The basis of present British Labour policy is not Marxian or Webbian, but Keynesian.' (See his 'Socialist Thought in Great Britain', *American Economic Review*, June 1957.) However, Professor Homan may be over-optimistic in his conclusion that 'the day of the prophetic Utopian vision, equally with the day of the Marxist imperative, appears to be over (presumably in Great Britain as well as in the United States).'

other economies with fairly stable demand but without sufficient domestic resources or sufficient foreign-exchange reserves. The chances of the American economic revolution succeeding along Keynesian lines are greater than critics of Keynesian policies are willing to admit, for, despite the limitations discussed above, parliamentary body politic, common suffrage, social security programmes, collective bargaining, mass education and other social-democratic practices in the United States are likely to give effect to more far-reaching social and economic reforms than anyone could have thought possible during the last century. The necessary reservation to have here is that the American economy may go beyond what Professor Hansen's mixed-economy, welfare-state approach would allow: (*a*) if moderate Keynesian policies prove inadequate to the task of maintaining stable growth, and (*b*) if other predominantly private-enterprise economies adopt, for economic or political reasons, more drastic programmes than Keynes intended for 'the democracy of nations'.

It may be true that the American economy has become less susceptible to instability, not in spite but because of Professor Hansen's 'stagnation thesis' and his anti-stagnation policy recommendations, as his book seems to imply. But it would be amiss for anyone to infer that therefore the essentially unstable nature of a predominantly market economy has disappeared. That cyclical growth is the essential way in which capitalism develops seems to remain as valid today as when Schumpeter held it in his day. The success of the American economic revolution based on Keynesian theory and policies will depend increasingly on future progress 'toward a blurring of the distinction between capitalism and other systems', toward that blurring process which is attributed to 'the influence of the Keynesian school'.[1] For both the romantic sympathy for 'capitalism' and the doctrinaire support of 'socialism' must give way to an elastic realism, if the mixed-economy, welfare-state approach is to be given full play, to experiment with social and economic reforms boldly and imaginatively. A modern mixed economy undergoing the Keynesian Revolution has the unique opportunity to demonstrate the wisdom of planning for stability and growth 'whilst preserving efficiency and freedom'[2] and on the basis of clear and perceptive recognition of the limitations which that economy itself occasions.

[1] See D. M. Wright, 'The Prospects for Capitalism', *A Survey of Contemporary Economics* (H. S. Ellis, ed.), 1948.

[2] Keynes, *General Theory*, p. 381.

CHAPTER 3

GOVERNOR ROCKEFELLER ON AMERICA'S ECONOMIC GROWTH*

As you know, 'to grow faster or not to grow faster' became an important campaign issue during the 1960 American Presidential election. As a matter of fact, the American controversy over faster economic growth had started before the Presidential election campaign as an *intra*-party rather than inter-party issue. For Governor Nelson A. Rockefeller started the controversy by publicly advocating 'accelerated economic growth' as 'a key to the American future'[1] and by subsequently provoking former Vice-President Richard Nixon into dismissing it as mere 'growth-manship'. Ironically the then Opposition Party came to Governor Rockefeller's rescue and adopted 'accelerated economic growth' as its own platform plank. This American political controversy is, I think, a reflection not only of the growth-conscious postwar world but also of the underlying and continuing disagreement among American economists on the goal and means of faster economic growth.

For in the United States, perhaps more than in any other mature nations, the tradition of static economics is waging a mortal struggle against the ascendance of what Sir Roy Harrod christened 'dynamic economics'. This professional struggle finds its pedestrian expression in the journalistic juxtaposition of 'price stability' with 'accelerated economic growth' as if they were hopelessly incompatible with each other. It is, therefore, no accident that one group of policy makers is so satisfied with the 'affluent' *status quo* as to reject faster growth as entailing more central planning and inflationary financing, while the other group advocates it both as a matter of national survival in an age of competitive international power politics and as an indispensable preliminary to greater material and spiritual wellbeing all around.

* My address to the Oxford Economic Society, at Nuffield College, Oxford, March 3, 1961—subsequently published as 'The American Controversy over Accelerated Economic Growth—A Post-Keynesian View', *Economic Studies Quarterly* (joint organ of the Japanese Economic Association and the Japanese Econometric Society), September 1961.

[1] See Gov. N. A. Rockefeller, *Accelerated Economic Growth—A Key to the American Future* (originally delivered as an address to the Governor's Conference on Automation, Cooperstown, New York, June 1, 1960).

I mention all this not only to provide some perspective but to relate my talk to both Governor Rockefeller's aforementioned report and post-Keynesian dynamic economics. However, I should like to concentrate on the Rockefeller report, since it is more pertinent to the American controversy under discussion. May I presume that you will draw some useful inferences from my critical observations for your own growth analysis and policy.

Let us first look at some growth rates which the American economy has achieved absolutely and in relation to other economies, and then examine the various reasons advanced for its faster growth in the decades ahead.

TABLE 1
*US Historical Growth Rates**
(Annual Averages)

Period	*GNP Growth Rate*
1869–1930	3.75%
1929–1939 (Great Depression)	0
1940–1945 (World War II)	10
1947–1960 (Postwar)	4

TABLE 2
Comparative Growth Rates†
(1950–57 Averages)

Country	*GNP Growth Rate*
Japan	8.5%
West Germany	8
USSR	6
Canada, France, Netherlands, Italy and Mexico	5
USA	4

* Adapted from the data in Gov. Rockefeller, *Accelerated Economic Growth*, etc. The growth rates cited by him presumably refer to 'real' and 'gross' figures.
† *Ibid.*

Table 1 raises the interesting question as to whether or not the American economy will be able to grow at a positive constant rate by avoiding serious depressions or at as steady and high a rate of 10 per cent in peacetime as it actually did in wartime. No less interesting is the question raised by Table 2, namely: will the American economy be able to grow as rapidly as the Japanese and German economies or faster than the Soviet economy in the coming decades?

Governor Rockefeller's own answer to these questions is that the American economy could and should grow as fast, if not faster, for reasons that remain controversial. He cites 'two compelling reasons' for faster growth, viz, the mounting national defence and welfare needs, and the intensifying international power struggle.[1] For the purpose of critical discussion these two reasons may be divided into three criteria, that is, (*a*) the *welfare* criterion, (*b*) the *defence* criterion, and (*c*) the *balance-of-power* criterion.

Increased welfare expenditure as a criterion of faster growth has the wide support of American economists and especially Professors A. H. Hansen and J. K. Galbraith[2] who have been most vocal in lamenting over 'the paradox of public squalor in the midst of private opulence', to borrow the phrase of Professor A. Schlesinger Jr.[3] Few would quarrel with Governor Rockefeller's plea for 'rising standards', 'better housing', 'improved educational opportunities' and 'improved individual security and job opportunities'[4] as valid grounds for more rapid economic growth, though some would question his tacit assumption that all this could be done 'within the framework of our existing system of initiative and enterprise'.[5]

But when it comes to his defence and balance-of-power criteria, we find a great deal of disagreement. In the first place, we find Professor P. A. Baran, of Stanford University, sharply criticizing a pseudo-patriotic tendency to equate general economic growth with the particular expansion of 'the gross national product's military component'.[6] Such a perverse tendency is, in Professor Baran's view, strengthened by advancing 'the Soviet challenge' as 'the reason for the necessity to accelerate the growth of the American economy'.[7] Governor Rockefeller is not entirely free from this sort of criticism, since he not only specifies 'cold war tensions' as his reason for advocating increased 'national security expenditures' but also stresses the balance-of-power necessity of counteracting the impression which the rapid Soviet growth rate may make on the underdeveloped nations that 'the Soviet system is better for promoting the economic growth these nations seek'.[8] On this score, however,

[1] Rockefeller, *op. cit.*, p. 9.

[2] See Hansen, *The American Economy*, 1957, and Galbraith, *The Affluent Society*, 1958.

[3] See Schlesinger, 'A Democratic View of the Republicans', *New York Times Magazine*, July 17, 1960 (under the main title 'The Two Parties: Two Viewpoints').

[4] Rockefeller, *Ibid.*

[5] *Ibid.*, p. 6. As if to anticipate such scepticism, Gov. Rockefeller adds the qualifying phrase '. . . with government action in a complementary and never a dominating role.' (*Ibid.*)

[6] See Baran, 'Problem of Achieving and Maintaining a High Rate of Economic Growth', *American Economic Review*, May 1960.

[7] *Ibid.*

[8] Rockefeller, *op. cit.*, pp. 10–11.

Governor Rockefeller has the academic support of Professor A. Bergson, of the Harvard University Russian Research Centre, who publicized the Soviet challenge as a necessary 'point of departure for any responsible formulation of our (American) own policies'.[1] My own feeling is that if the Soviet challenge were stressed rather more as the *sputnik* type of scientific and educational competition, it would have a salutary effect on the nature and direction of American economic growth programmes.

Finally, the defence and balance-of-power criteria are subject to yet another line of criticism, for Governor Rockefeller's reference to America's wartime growth performance and his inference that 'the American economy can respond superbly to challenge'[2] may unintentionally encourage another perverse tendency to create or maintain a warlike atmosphere as the most expedient impetus to faster growth. It is instructive, in this respect, that the postwar Japanese economy, whose 8.5 per cent rate of growth Governor Rockefeller approvingly cites as an instance of 'free economies' achieving 'rates of economic advance that outstrip the Soviet record',[3] has been criticized by Professor S. Tsuru as tending to rely too precariously on the 'circumstances of war or warlike situation'.[4] Intellectual precaution against such perverse tendencies as mentioned above cannot be emphasized too strongly, if the American economy is to be spared the avoidable charge that it cannot and will not achieve prosperity and growth without warlike activities and proclivities.

From the vantage point of post-Keynesian growth analysis and experience I should now like to call your attention to the following analytical weaknesses in Governor Rockefeller's valiant attempt to 'examine what forces and measures can be mastered to achieve that growth'.[5]

In singling out 'high investment' as the most strategic determinant of 'rapid economic growth'[6] Governor Rockefeller completely ignores the sort of difficulties arising from the dual nature of investment stressed by post-Keynesian economists on both sides of the Atlantic. Consider, for example, the implications of the familiar Harrod-Domar conditions:[7]

[1] See his letter to the editors of *The New York Times*, October 16, 1960.

[2] Rockefeller, *op. cit.*, p. 6.

[3] *Ibid.*, p. 11.

[4] See Tsuru, 'The Strength and Weakness of Japanese Economy', in *Essays on the Japanese Economy*, 1958.

[5] Rockefeller, *op. cit.*, p. 5.

[6] *Ibid.*, pp. 12–13.

[7] See R. F. Harrod, *Towards a Dynamic Economics*, and also his 'Domar and

$$\Delta Y = \frac{s}{C_r} Y; \frac{\Delta Y}{Y} = \frac{s}{C_r}, \text{ (Harrod)} \qquad (1)$$

$$\frac{\Delta I}{\alpha} = \sigma I; \frac{\Delta I}{I} = \alpha\sigma, \qquad \text{(Domar)} \qquad (2)$$

Here Y is net real national income (demanded or supplied), I net investment, C_r the equilibrium or required capital coefficient (Harrod), *s* the saving ratio (Harrod), σ investment productivity (Domar; the reciprocal of Harrod's C_r on some assumption), and α the saving ratio (Domar; the marginal counterpart of Harrod's average saving ratio). In the basic equations given by (1) and (2), the left-hand side represents national income or effective demand while the right-hand side represents productive capacity or effective supply, though there are some different points of detail between them. The derived rate of growth of income ($\Delta Y/Y$) due to Harrod implies the derived rate of growth of net investment *à la* Domar ($\Delta I/I$)—on favourable assumptions. The former implies that if the actual rate of growth of income exceeds the equilibrium rate of growth of productive capacity, $(\Delta Y/Y) > (s/C_r)$, the resulting trend will be inflationary. The latter implies that if the actual rate of growth of net investment-demand exceeds the equilibrium rate of growth of capital stock, $(\Delta I/I) > (\alpha\sigma)$, the consequential trend will be also inflationary. Mass unemployment will be the logical outcome if the sign is reversed in both cases of inequalities.

In the post-Keynesian world where supply is no longer assumed to create its own demand, it is essential that we take due cognizance of a possible conflict between the *income-generating effect* of investment and its *capacity-increasing effect*. The only way to get around such a conflict would be by assuming dubiously that the 'high investment' needed for faster growth consists wholly of the armaments or pyramid-building variety that expands income without at the same time expanding capacity. The Harrod-Domar conditions are important to satisfy because the growth of effective demand, however fast initially, would be reversed if productive capacity failed to keep pace with the former growth, just as the rapid growth of productive capacity would sooner or later be arrested if effective demand failed to grow as fast.

In projecting a 5 per cent or 6 per cent growth rate for the target year (1970), Governor Rockefeller tacitly assumes that the growth parameters involved will remain the same as in the beginning or base year (1960). But if the parameters change between the target

Dynamic Economics', *Economic Journal*, September 1959; E. Domar, *Essays in the Theory of Economic Growth*, 1957, esp. Chapters 3 and 4.

year and the base year, the realized growth rate will differ from its predicted value significantly, as the empirical testing of forecasting growth models has revealed in many instances. It seems more useful to view a target rate of growth as something to be achieved by deliberate public policy rather than as something to be predicted under *laissez-faire*. Thus viewed, parametric estimates could be based on such dynamic policy assumptions as

$$\frac{s_{t+1}}{s_t}=1+\beta, \tag{3}$$

and

$$\frac{b_{t+1}}{b_t}=1-\gamma. \tag{4}$$

Here s is the saving ratio, b the capital coefficient, β the rate of increase in the saving ratio, γ the rate of decrease in the capital coefficient, t the base year of the programming horizon envisaged, and $t+1$ the target year (as when the annual average growth rate is desired). Assumptions (3) and (4) imply a higher target rate of growth than in the past decade:

$$g=\frac{Y_{t+1}}{Y_t}-1=\frac{s_{t+1}}{b_{t+1}}=\frac{s_t\,(1+\beta)}{b_t(1-\gamma)}, \tag{5}$$

where Y is net real national income, g the programmed rate of growth of real net national income over the whole programming horizon (e.g. 50 per cent in a ten-year growth programme, or 5 per cent per year[1]), and the other variables the same as before. Equation (5) expresses the programming version of Sir Roy Harrod's 'warranted' rate of growth.

It is doubtful that 'automation' and 'modernization', which Governor Rockefeller favours as part of *private* enterprise,[2] are sufficient to increase the productivity of investment and so to decrease the capital coefficient over time. To warrant assumption (4), it would be necessary to adopt a conscious and vigorous *public* policy of increasing investment productivity. It would be even more necessary to adopt a public policy of increasing the saving ratio secularly, as assumption (3) implies, especially in view of the fact that there are in the American economy such powerful trend forces

[1] Though not in the published version, I might add the computational method:

$$\left(1+\frac{G}{n}\right)^{nt}=(1+g)^{t+n}, \qquad (t=0, 1, 2, \ldots, n)$$

$$Y_{t+n}=\lim_{\substack{n\to\infty \\ \Delta Y\to 0}}\sum_{t}^{t+n} Y_t(1+g)^{t+n}=\int_t^{t+n} Y_t e^{gt}dt=G\int_0^n Y_t e^{Gt}dt,$$

where G is the rate of growth over n years.

[2] Rockefeller, *op. cit.*, pp. 3, 13.

tending to decrease the saving ratio as social-security programmes, consumer credit systems, and progressive tax structures. Thus, if the key parameters s and b are treated as *policy parameters*, the growth of the American economy can be greatly more accelerated than in conditions largely of *laissez-faire*.

I wish to close this talk by expressing my hope that the current practice of bickering and 'politiking' over so-called 'growth-manship' will be soon over. For that practice is based on the unwarranted innuendo that those espousing 'accelerated economic growth' (presumably including Governor Rockefeller) are all rascals in favour of central planning and inflationary development—as if the rapid growth of productivity were not the ultimate and non-partisan antidote for both demand-pull and cost-push inflations as well as a prerequisite to liberty, variety, gaiety and other advantages of traditional individualism which Keynes stressed so pregnantly and poignantly.[1]

[1] *General Theory*, pp. 380–1.

CHAPTER 4

THE 'PRINCIPIA ETHICA' OF AN AFFLUENT SOCIETY*

Sir Roy Harrod once wrote to me: 'Now that we are growing richer —take the US, for example—we can afford to think of the use of leisure and what sweetens that use. It won't be nice if people think of nothing but eating or driving cars about.'[1] He anticipated the kind of self-criticism that Kenneth Galbraith was to hurl so refreshingly against his own economic society with its passions for big bank balances, split-level ranch houses, and fancy tail fins.[2] Both Harrod's above remark and Galbraith's lament in turn are reminiscent of Keynes's hopeful and exhortative criticism of 'irreligious Capitalism'.[3] I should like in this short essay to outline the 'principa ethica' (to borrow G. E. Moore's expression for the philosophy of general conduct that had an abiding influence on Keynes)[4] of an affluent society—in the light of Keynesian and post-Keynesian insights. Such an outline may be found useful in our increasingly important efforts to 'reap spiritual fruits from our material conquests'.[5]

We have been disciplined to strive in peace and to die in war so long that it will not be easy to live in order to enjoy or to enjoy in order to live when the opportunity comes. Since general affluence

* Originally appeared under the same title in *The American Journal of Economics and Sociology*, April 1962.

[1] Harrod's letter to the author is dated April 26, 1950.

[2] See Galbraith, *The Affluent Society* (Boston: Houghton Mifflin, 1958). Perhaps 'self-criticism' is not so perspicuous a term to describe his book, since Galbraith was born in Canada and hence is in a better position to criticize the American economy objectively.

[3] See his *Essays in Persuasion* (London: Rupert Hart-Davis, 1952), p. 307.

[4] Cf. J. M. Keynes, 'My Early Beliefs', in *Two Memoirs* (London: Rupert Hart-Davis, 1949). This is not to suggest that Keynes agreed wholly with Moore's social ethics, since the former sought a more pragmatic and less transcendental 'principle of organic unity' than was found in the latter's teachings. Nevertheless, Keynes shared Moore's fundamental sense of value, for he believed with Moore that 'love, the creation and enjoyment of aesthetic experience and the pursuit of knowledge' are one's supreme objects in life, and that 'of these love came a long way first'. (*Ibid.*, p. 83.)

[5] Keynes made this remark in his review of H. G. Wells's *The World of William Glissold*, which review was subsequently reproduced in his *Persuasion* (esp. p. 354).

may arrive sooner than we think, it would be fruitful to rediscipline ourselves to live 'wisely and agreeably' in the new affluent world to come, as Keynes precautioned.[1] The *modus operandi* of this new living would require a higher scale of values than that which obtains at present. Let us begin our search for a new scale of values by reference to Keynes's digressive allusion to 'non-economic purposes', 'the art of life' and 'other matters of greater and more permanent significance'.[2] We may discuss the matter under several headings.

Social Amenity. An affluent society can and must be characterized by greater sensibilities toward the amenity value of things and persons. Freedom from importunate economic necessities sets the stage for a holiday mood, for sheer pleasure without business, for a permanent sense of wellbeing and security, for genuine urbanity and suavity, for pure arts and sciences, and for many other pleasantries. Today these pleasantries are by and large a monopoly of the so-called 'leisure class', but tomorrow people may all behave like ladies and gentlemen of leisure as a matter of course. For in the coming universe of general affluence no 'snub value' is likely to be attached to long nails and small feet, as in the aristocratic and plutocratic mores of ancient China, since all will be in a position to have them.

A bit of this is already seen in the United States, where remarkable mass production coupled with high mass purchasing power is having the effect of gradually destroying the traditional prestige value attached to Cadillacs, mansions, 'Ivy League' private schools, and exclusive resorts—much to the dismay and distress of *nouveaux riches*, fourflushers and masqueraders. Veblen's concept of 'conspicuous consumption' is fast becoming meaningless in an age of mass production and credit-living, in spite of the monopolistic competitors' frantic attempts at 'product differentiation' (an inelastic demand curve for the economist but a pressure device to induce prestige-conscious consumers to keep up with the Joneses and to keep ahead of the Smiths, actually). No wonder that Galbraith has chosen to entitle his book *The Affluent Society*, although America may cease to enjoy the unique distinction of being *the* affluent society in a foreseeable future. No wonder, either, that Miss Lotus Blossom (the Japanese *geisha* girl of the cinema *The Tea House of the August Moon*) should be interpreted by Sakini (*à la* Marlon Brando) as expressing her desire to go to America, where 'people let the machines do all the work so that they can sit around to sip tea all day'!

It would be amiss, however, not to mention certain difficulties involved in the transition to a life of ease and comfort, to a push-

[1] *Persuasion*, p. 367.
[2] *Ibid.*, pp. 365 ff.

button automation age of short working hours. Leisure with income but without the know-how to occupy it could mean boredom and at worst a nervous breakdown, as Keynes warned.[1] People without such know-how might easily fall victims to neurosis, alcoholism, eroticism, and other dissipations, as is already observable in some wealthy quarters of the world. Still, with a little training and ambition, people surely will be able to find many more things amusing and absorbing than the leisure class of today seems able to find. Adult-education programmes, such as some American and European universities now offer, seem to provide a splendid opportunity to acquire the know-how to occupy usefully and pleasantly the increasing leisure made available by an affluent society. Otherwise we might find ourselves thinking of 'nothing but eating or driving cars about'.

Cultural Elegance. Another human value of permanent importance to grace an affluent society would be cultural elegance in the sense that the community possesses the discernment and refinement of taste acquired through intellectual and aesthetic upbringing. Subjective notions of what constitutes excellent taste may differ widely, but whatever the best judgment of the community decides to be in excellent taste represents the fittest, the most beautiful, and the most orderly in form and expression to be found in any period or place. This quality of life is almost confined today to a small group of individuals in whose veins blue blood runs, who were born with silver spoons in their mouths, and who were discretely trained to discern and appreciate that quality. But the general affluence of tomorrow would enable the majority of mankind to possess that cultural quality as their common property, instead of fatalistically viewing it as the exclusive monopoly of the few.

It is interesting, in this respect, to compare Keynes and Schumpeter. Brought up against the backgrounds of Eton, Cambridge and Bloomsbury, reinforced by his own fame and fortune, Keynes personally exemplified cultural elegance to the *n*th degree. A more spectacular instance was seen in Joseph Schumpeter, whose elegant taste was sometimes jestingly exaggerated by reference to his dislike for 'a civilization of Coca-Cola and Mickey Mouse'. The difference between the two economists on this score, though, is that Schumpeter apparently considered cultural elegance as the permanent and exclusive property of the 'chosen' few, while Keynes regarded it as a desideratum for all mankind, especially in the coming age of general affluence. One might add the conjecture that Lady Keynes probably had a great deal to do with Keynes's growing conviction that one justification for wanting and having money lies in spending it for the

[1] *Ibid.*, pp. 366–7.

ballet and such elegant entertainment at will, judging from Sir Roy Harrod's description of 'the exquisite ballerina'.[1]

General affluence would facilitate the observance of the proprieties and the development of excellent taste. For those who possess the will to have the best of everything would possess also the necessary means, while those lacking the means could develop the will. In the meantime some people might find themselves inadvertently confusing exquisite taste with expensive taste or equating elegant manners with arrogant manners. Perhaps a larger cut of the national income pie should be allocated than at present to the systematic cultivation of good taste. With deliberate intellectual and aesthetic training through the modern media of mass education and mass communication, a high standard of living would represent also more graceful living all around.

Intellectual Excellence. The optimal allocation of human resources for cultural progress in general and for effective statesmanship in particular presupposes a permanent system of priority allocations based on demonstrated intellectual efficiency. A society putting a premium on mediocrity and conformity would be considered as malallocating human resources from a Keynesian point of view. For Keynes would give 'unhindered opportunity to the exceptional and to the aspiring'.[2]

It is interesting, in this regard, to distinguish Keynes's view of the elite from that of Plato. The elite in Plato's sense seems to refer to a hereditary intelligentsia with presumably innate insight into the transcendental values of 'Beauty, Truth and Goodness' to be supported by a permanent stratum of slaves; to gentlemen and scholars who can literally live and think in Ivory Tower by virtue of their aristocratic birth and owing to a slavery that attends to all the mundane chores. Ironically, what the sociologist calls 'the power elite' of a modern society seems to express the spirit of the Platonic elite. By contrast, the elite in Keynes's sense refers to an 'intellectual aristocracy'[3] whose quest of 'love, beauty and truth'[4] is not for the sake of those values in the abstract but for the concrete good of those to be governed by persuasion, and whose creative activity is to be facilitated by general consent and affluence.

There is one thing more about Keynes' view of intellectualism that needs special emphasis. And that is his preachment and practice of combining 'affection and reason', a unique combination the absence

[1] See his *The Life of John Maynard Keynes* (New York: Harcourt, Brace, 1951).
[2] *Persuasion*, p. 344.
[3] See Harrod, *The Life of John Maynard Keynes*, p. 192.
[4] See footnote 4, p. 44, in this connection.

of which in many people he subtly deplored by quoting Shelley: 'The wise lack love, and those who love lack wisdom.'[1] Intellectual genius without the human touch could be as dangerous as supersonic speed without the wisdom to direct it. Keynes's concept of intellectual excellence therefore carries with it the implication that there should be an intelligentsia with a heart and a synthesis of scientific analysis and value judgment. It also implies that a social policy of fostering intellectual excellence ought to require such minimal steps as guaranteed academic freedom, discerning systems of honours and awards based on merit, scholarly grants and aids irrespective of race, colour and social origin, and tax concessions and other public inducements to scholarship. Beyond such specifics, there is a general need to heed Schumpeter's well-known warning that a failure to show a greater respect for the intellectual would provoke such intellectual resentment as to contribute to the downfall of materially successful yet anti-intellectual society.[2]

Altruistic Individualism. The last of the higher human values to be sketched is a paradoxical one of altruistic individualism. Keynes, while he was 'an individualist to the finger-tips', nevertheless had the social sensibility to believe in the desirability and possibility of 'planning and contriving' for the welfare of his fellow men, as Sir Roy Harrod movingly tells us.[3] We are also told that Keynes reconciled his 'adamant and uncompromising individualism' with his 'fervent belief in planning' by choosing and specializing in economics—a field that essentially offers a creative opportunity to do something tangible for others. Keynes in his turn tells us this of Alfred Marshall: '. . . it was through Ethics that he first reached Economics.'[4] However, Keynes's *General Theory*, unlike Marshall's *Principles*, not only demonstrated the futility and calamity of rugged individualism in the economic field but also suggested a new experiment in the macroeconomic art of mixing individual initiative and social planning, private profit-making and public responsibility, and personal liberty and collective wisdom.

If a mixed public-private economy of the Keynesian type represents also a permanently prosperous society, the general observance of altruistic individualism will become that much easier. For it is less difficult to practise enlightened selfishness or to live up to social

[1] As related by J. T. Sheppard in *John Maynard Keynes, 1883–1946* (Council of King's College).

[2] See his *Capitalism, Socialism and Democracy* in general and his 'The March into Socialism', *American Economic Review* (May 1950), in particular.

[3] *Op. cit.*, pp. 191–2.

[4] *Keynes, Essays in Biography* (New York: Horizon Press, 1951), p. 137.

responsibility in an affluent society than in an indigent society, as experience and observation abundantly testify. The only important exception to this rule can be seen in the traditional and continuing case of religionists who are dedicated to the cause of altruism as a matter of course, despite their material austerity and irrespective of pecuniary rewards. Such an exception may well become rather general, not because people would become more religious, but because the milieu of general affluence would render altruism more practicable.

Altruistic individualism in the *economic* field implies the end of the old assumption that individual economic interests are 'naturally' above social control and the beginning of the new assumption that 'the greatest happiness of the greatest number' is best served by a proper blending of public guidance and private initiative; the end of money-making and money-loving as the main motive of individual economic actions and the beginning of altruistic impulses as the dominant factor in productive, creative activities. Altruistic individualism in *extra-economic* areas implies, at least, the stimulation of independent thinking tempered by the free exchange of ideas; the encouragement of individual variety in taste and choice expressed in a socially agreeable manner; a greater social respect for privacy; and the guarantee of the civil liberties and rights of individuals coupled with their discharge of public obligations and responsibilities. The new individualism, as such, will gradually replace the old traditional individualism *pari passu* with growing and spreading affluence, while simultaneously exercising a liberalizing influence on the extreme collectivist societies as well.

Such are, to repeat, 'non-economic purposes', 'the art of life' and 'other matters of greater and more permanent significance' to which Keynes alluded, and which post-Keynesian thinking must implement if economic affluence is to be meaningful in terms of human values.

PART II

PROBLEMS OF DEVELOPING ECONOMIES

CHAPTER 5

A LINEAR PROGRAMMING MODEL OF GROWTH WITHOUT AUSTERITY*

Classical economists made economic progress in general and capital formation in particular a function of 'the abstinence of the rich', implying inequality as a *sine qua non*. This traditional 'abstinence' doctrine finds its modern expression in various national programmes of austerity (as enforced by rationing, priority resource allocation, consumption taxes, consumer-credit control, and selective import quotas—even in peacetime). Such austerity programmes based on the 'abstinence' doctrine is naturally unpalatable to capital-poor yet welfare-conscious economies, especially when those economies are exposed, via the international 'demonstration effect', to the higher consumption standards of affluent economies.

Fortunately, however, Keynes and Schumpeter have left with us such insights as would enable developing economies to escape from the supposed necessity of austerity. I refer to Keynes's daring proposals for domestic 'loan expenditure' and the multinational financing of postwar development (via the World Bank which was his brain-child) on the one hand,[1] and, on the other hand, to Schumpeter's sweeping espousal of 'credit' as one of the triagonal prerequisites of economic development (the other two being familiarly 'innovation' and 'entrepreneurship').[2]

I should like in this paper[3] to build a linear programming model of optimal growth for underdeveloped economies in the light of the

* Originally published under the same title in *Indian Journal of Economics*, April 1963.

[1] *General Theory*, especially where Keynes refers to 'a growing class of investments entered upon by, or at the risk of, public authorities, which are frankly influenced in making the investment by a general presumption of there being perspective social advantages from the investment' (p. 163), and to 'the net borrowing of public authorities on all accounts, whether on capital account or to meet a budgetary deficit' (pp. 128–9); and Opening Remarks at the First Meeting of the Second Commission on the World Bank, July 3, 1944.

[2] *The Theory of Economic Development*, 1934.

[3] This is an outcome of my research on mathematical programming and dynamic economics at the Oxford University Institute of Statistics in Spring 1961. In that connection I had stimulating discussions with Sir Roy Harrod, Professor J. R. Hicks, Mr I. M. D. Little, Mr E. F. Jackson and Mr P. Streeten.

aforementioned insights of Keynes and Schumpeter, and in the perspective of postwar experience[1]—with a view to illustrating the theoretical possibility of those economies growing rapidly without imposing austerity on the already austere (poverty-stricken in some extreme cases) community.

For this purpose let us make the *institutional* assumptions (*a*) that the underdeveloped economy in question lacks a highly developed capital market to facilitate the equity and debt financing of investment or a widespread corporate policy of reinvesting undistributed profits; (*b*) that it nevertheless possesses, among other financial agencies, government-managed development banks that are specifically designed to help finance private investment in plant and equipment; (*c*) that its government investment is confined to social overheads (transportation and communications facilities, highways, harbours, dams, and the like) and financed by public borrowing on capital account, and from the central bank[2] (government consumption expenditure being held constantly equal to taxes, *ex hypothesi*); and (*d*) that its capital imports are not only developmental in character but also of an autonomous and anonymous nature[3] (e.g. from the World Bank), instead of a compensatory nature based on the arbitrary import surpluses financed by *laissez-faire* capital imports or by unilateral foreign borrowing. In addition, let us make the *analytical* assumptions (*a*′) that the underdeveloped economy has redundant material and human resources that normally remain unmobilized for lack of capital funds;[4] (*b*′) that it is disaggregatable into

[1] Japan's credit-stimulated post-war growth is the most spectacular instance. In this connection, see M. Shinohara, *Growth and Cycles in the Japanese Economy*, 1962; K. K. Kurihara, 'Observations on Japan's Ten-Year Growth Plan', *Kyklos*, Vol. XV, 1962. I had rather confirmatory conversations with Professors K. Ohkawa and I. Yamada, both of Hitotsubashi University, during their recent visits to the United States. For other instances see S. Ghosh, *The Financing of Economic Development*, 1962; P. Hasan, *Deficit Financing and Capital Formation*, 1962.

[2] It may be presumed that the resulting public debt is paid off by the government out of the profits of the central bank and other government-owned banks largely accruing to the government itself. On this presumption, no such tax burden as is usually associated with the payment of maturing public debts would stem from this type of public borrowing. This method of deficit financing seems more justifiable *on capital account* than on current account, though not much more if the current account includes greater *welfare expenditure* than can be financed by taxes alone.

[3] The conventional 'transfer' problem is of marginal importance in the present context of a borrowing yet growing economy, especially since developmental loans of a multinational nature are extended on rather liberal terms, as the lending policy of the World Bank has admirably demonstrated.

[4] It is the *volume* of capital funds, not capital-charges (interest rates), that is

four conceptual sectors, namely: the private saving-investment sector, the domestic private borrowing-investment sector, the foreign private borrowing-investment sector, and the government borrowing-investment sector—according to the sources of investible resources; and (*c′*) that both aggregate and sectoral investments are linearly related to corresponding outputs during the programming horizon envisaged (the shorter is the horizon, the greater will be the plausibility of the linearity assumption).

On these assumptions, the 'savings-investment' relation can take the equilibrium form

(1) $$S_p+D_g+B_d+B_f=I_p+I_g+L_d+L_f,$$

where S_p is private savings, D_g government deficit borrowing on capital account, B_d domestic borrowing (from the development banks), B_f foreign autonomous borrowing (from, e.g., the World Bank), I_p private net investment, I_g government net investment, L_d domestic lending (through capital markets), and L_f foreign autonomous lending (through the central bank, export-import banks, and other inter-governmental financial agencies). It seems safe to presume that L_d and L_f are quantitatively insignificant in the specifically long-run context of an underdeveloped economy, though there are some short-run exceptions. Equation (1) reveals the possibility of there being always $I_p+I_g>S_p$ by an amount equal to $D_g+(B_d-L_d)+(B_f-L_f)$ in the circumstances described by our institutional and analytical assumptions *supra*.

Let those variables of equation (1) enter into the following structural parameters:

(2) $$s=S_p/Y,$$
(3) $$b=(I_p+I_g)/\Delta Y,$$
(4) $$\delta=\overline{D}_g/Y,$$
(5) $$\beta_d=B_d/Y,$$
(6) $$\beta_f=\overline{B}_f/Y,$$
(7) $$\mu_d=L_d/Y,$$
(8) $$\mu_f=\overline{L}_f/Y.$$

Here Y is net national output or productive capacity (in contradistinction to effective demand), *s* the average private propensity to save, *b* the average-marginal capital coefficient (on the assumption

relevant here, though some private investors may still be sensitive to interest change—judging from the Japanese experience referred to above. Needless to say, public investment is generally interest-inelastic. Furthermore, those investments which might be financed by domestic and foreign borrowing would not, as some writers fear, necessarily increase inflationary pressures inasmuch as the investments involved here are specified as a *capacity-increasing* variety (instead of being just an income-generating variety, as in the case of pyramid-building).

of $(K_p+K_g)/Y=\text{const.}$ and $I_p+I_g=\Delta K_p+\Delta K_g$, where K is fixed real capital), δ the ratio of government deficit borrowing to national output, β_d the average domestic propensity to borrow, β_f the ratio of foreign autonomous borrowing to national output, μ_d the average domestic propensity to lend, and μ_f the ratio of foreign autonomous lending to national output, all other variables being the same as before.

Taking (2)–(8) into account, we can rewrite equation (1) as

$$\text{(9)} \qquad b\Delta Y=sY+\delta Y+\beta_d Y+\beta_f Y-\mu_d Y-\mu_f Y,$$

dividing both sides of which by bY yields the rate of growth of net national output (*g*):

$$\text{(10)} \qquad g=\frac{\Delta Y}{Y}=\frac{s+\delta+\beta_d+\beta_f-\mu_d-\mu_f}{b}$$
$$=\frac{s+(\beta_d-\mu_d)+(\beta_f-\mu_f)+\delta}{b}.$$

Equation (1) thus reveals the relative contributions which private saving, domestic net borrowing, foreign net borrowing, and government deficit borrowing are capable of making to the overall growth rate in terms of ratios, when the capital-output ratio remains constant.

On the above-mentioned parenthetical assumption regarding the relation of K and Y and that of I and ΔK, we may bring out the implication of equation (10) for capital growth:

$$\text{(11)} \qquad g=\frac{\frac{S_p+(B_d-L_d)+(B_f-L_f)+D_g}{Y}}{\frac{K}{Y}}=\frac{\frac{I_p+I_g}{Y}}{\frac{K}{Y}}=\frac{\frac{\Delta K}{Y}}{\frac{K}{Y}}=\frac{\Delta K}{K},$$

where ΔK/K is the rate of growth of real capital. Thus the rate of growth of net national output given by (10) implies the same rate of growth of capital.

So far our analysis has been made in aggregative terms without explicitly showing the mechanism of sectoral contributions. Not only that, but the growth rate given by (10) cannot be regarded as a maximand or an optimand unless a target (or objective) function is specified, and until boundary conditions (constraints, so-called) are explicitly imposed on the solution of the problem in hand. This is where linear programming[1] comes to the rescue.

[1] For alternative applications of linear programming to dynamic economics see United Nations, *Programming Techniques for Economic Development*, 1960 (esp. appendices by Prof. S. Ichimura, of Osaka University, Japan); J. Tinbergen and H. C. Bos, *Mathematical Models of Economic Growth*, 1962; O. Lange, *Intro-*

Accordingly, let us now turn to a linear programming formulation of our growth problem. Suppose that the following are given as preassigned parameters:

$$(12)\quad \begin{cases} b_i = I_i/\Delta Y_i, & (i=1, \ldots, 4) \\ s = S_p/Y, & \\ \delta = \bar{D}_g/Y, & \\ \beta_d = B_d/Y, & \\ \beta_f = \bar{B}_f/Y, & \\ \mu_d = L_d/Y, & \\ \mu_f = \bar{L}_f/Y, & \\ \lambda_i = \Delta g/\Delta g_i. & (i=1, \ldots, 4) \end{cases}$$

Here b_i is the i-th sector's capital-output ratio, ΔY_i an increment of the i-th sector's net output, λ_i the marginal worth or utility of sectoral growth rates, the remainder being the same as before. λ_i's are sometimes called 'shadow prices' or 'valuations' by which the unknowns of a target function are to be weighted for different kinds of optimal programming. As such, λ_i's reflect certain priority considerations on the part of the policy-makers involved. Thus, for example, preassigning numerical values $\lambda_1=1$, $\lambda_2=1.7$, $\lambda_3=1.9$, and $\lambda_4=1.5$ would signify that the policy-makers consider it desirable to expect a smaller marginal contribution from the first sector relatively to those of the other sectors. For preassigning 1 (= base valuation) to the first sector implies that the policy-makers do not wish to change the prevailing pattern of consumption (i.e. not to effect any further national 'belt-tightening'), since the first sector's investment activity depends, given the sectoral capital-output ratios, on private saving, while the other sectors depend respectively on domestic borrowing, foreign borrowing, and government borrowing, as equation (10) shows.

Given the advance data specified by (12), maximize the linear target function of the form

$$(13)\quad \psi(g) = \sum_{i=1}^{n} \lambda_i g_i, \quad (\psi(\lambda g) = \lambda\psi(g) \text{ with respect to } \lambda)$$

subject to the constraints

$$(14)\quad b_1 g_1 \leqq s \text{ or } \frac{I_{p1}}{\Delta Y_1}\,\frac{\Delta Y_1}{Y_1} = \frac{I_{p1}}{Y_1} \leqq \frac{S_p}{Y},$$

duction to Econometrics, 1959; R. Dorfman, *et al.*, *Linear Programming and Economic Analysis*, 1958; and H. B. Chenery, *et al.*, *Studies in Linear and Non-Linear Programming* (Stanford), 1958.

(15) $$b_2g_2 \leqq \beta_d - \mu_d \text{ or } \frac{I_{p2}}{\Delta Y_2} \frac{\Delta Y_2}{Y_2} = \frac{I_{p2}}{Y_2} \leqq \frac{B_d}{Y} - \frac{L_d}{Y},$$

(16) $$b_3g_3 \leqq \beta_f - \mu_f \text{ or } \frac{I_{p3}}{\Delta Y_3} \frac{\Delta Y_3}{Y_3} = \frac{I_{p3}}{Y_3} \leqq \frac{\bar{B}_f}{Y} - \frac{\bar{L}_f}{Y},$$

(17) $$b_4g_4 \leqq \delta \text{ or } \frac{I_g}{\Delta Y_4} \frac{\Delta Y_4}{Y_4} = \frac{I_g}{Y_4} \leqq \frac{\bar{D}_g}{Y},$$

and

(18) $g_i \geqq 0$ for all i. $(i=1, \ldots, n;\ n=4)$

In this linear programming model, only one configuration of g_i's will maximize and optimize g for a given set of λ_i's.[1] Our problem here is one of seeking such values of n unknowns (g_i's) as would maximize the target function (12) while at the same time satisfying the requirements expressed by (14)–(18). When n linear inequalities are replaced by n equations (via non-negative 'slack variables'), we shall find n unknowns and thus a determinate solution in this model. The maximand as well as optimand g so determined represents the best possible path of growth, since it signifies that all the sectors are expanding their productive capacity by investing up to the limit set by the available supply of investible resources (mobilized respectively via private saving, domestic borrowing, foreign borrowing, and government deficit borrowing), as the constraints given by (14)–(17) indicate. The non-negativity requirements expressed by (18) are for the purpose of insuring a basic feasible solution (same number of non-negative variables as the number of equations) in the programming model. It is to be noted, also, that the right-hand indicator of equation (13) specifies the condition that must be satisfied in order to justify the linearity assumption involved in the target function.

To give emphasis to the sectoral roles of g_3 (due to foreign net autonomous borrowing, viz., from the World Bank and other multinational instrumentalities) and g_4 (due to government deficit borrowing on capital account) would be to follow the spirit of Keynes, while stressing the role of g_2 (due to domestic net borrowing, i.e. from the development banks in the present context) or the desideratum of $db_i/dt < 0$ (a lower sectoral capital-output ratio or a higher productivity of capital via innovation) would be in keeping with the spirit of Schumpeter, as our prefatory remarks imply. I have endeavoured to implement both the spirit of Keynes and the spirit of Schumpeter,

[1] It is presumed that the *target* value of g is set by reference to the economy's technological advance and population growth in a manner which I indicated elsewhere (*The Keynesian Theory of Economic Development*, esp. Chapter III on the socially optimal rate of growth), with a prospective view to making it coincide with the *programmed* value of g.

as such, in the light of post-Keynesian dynamic economics and mathematical programming, and in the specific interest of developing economies which would otherwise find themselves confronted with greater national belt-tightening and income inequality than might be deemed politically tolerable and ethically justifiable. The foregoing analysis may have justified the conclusion that developing economies need no longer follow, however sceptically, the classical 'abstinence of the rich' doctrine or adopt, however reluctantly, austerity programmes in order to develop their productive capacity and raise their living standards—especially in this day and age of the universal drive for greater equality, liberty and gaiety.

APPENDIX TO CHAPTER 5

JAPAN'S CREDIT-SUPPORTED GROWTH AND LINEAR PROGRAMMIMG

I should like in this appendix to implement my earlier reference to the Japanese economy's credit-supported growth (p. 54, n.1). For this purpose I propose to construct an illustrative macro model, and then offer the linear programming formulation of credit-supported growth both in multisectoral terms and matrix notation.

THE MACRO MODEL*

In a significant footnote to his controversial paper Dr H. Shimomura (of the Japanese government-owned Development Bank or *Nippon Kaihatsu Ginko*) reveals a key to Japan's high-saving, high-investment dynamics.[1] *There*, he urges such a dynamic financial policy as to enable Japan to liberate herself from the traditional static concept of saving-investment equilibrium, though he fails to demonstrate a functional relation between such a financial policy and the amazingly high target investment ratio of nearly 30 per cent envisaged in his growth model. We may approximate the operational possibility of the Shimomura model, thus:

Let the credit-creating Japanese economy have the following structural parameters and parametric values:

$$(1.1)\qquad \begin{cases} I/\Delta Y = b = 2.5, \\ S/Y \;= s = \;.15, \\ \bar{D}/Y \;= d = \;.1, \end{cases}$$

where Y is real national income or output, S private savings, I private net investment in fixed capital (plant and equipment), $\bar{D}$ autonomous long-term credit supplied by the banking system (including Shimomura's Development Bank and the Long-Term Credit Bank of Japan in the present context) for the specific purpose of financing private fixed invest-

* This section is a slightly modified part of my 'Observations on Japan's Ten-Year Growth Plan', *Kyklos*, Vol. XV, 1962.

[1] See H. Shimomura, 'Basic Problems of Growth Policy', *Economic Studies Quarterly*, March 1961, esp. n.9. In that paper Shimomura optimistically predicts a 10 per cent growth rate or more as an achievable and sustainable figure for the Japanese economy, whereas the Japanese Economic Planning Agency's *New Long-Range Economic Plan of Japan, 1961–70* (Government of Japan, 1958) and *Economic White Paper* (1961) rather more cautiously envisage an annual GNP growth rate of around 7.2 per cent as a plausible prospect in Japan for the coming decade.

ment, b the capital-output ratio (since $I=\Delta K$), s the saving ratio, and d the ratio of autonomous credit to national income considered as a fixed desideratum (and datum). The corresponding parametric values are not implausible if judged by the Japanese literature cited in this paper (see, in addition, Bank of Japan Economic Research Department, *Flow of Funds in the Japanese Economy during 1959*, Tokyo, 1960).

Taking (1.1) into account, we may equate the economy's aggregate induced investment to its aggregate 'savings' in the form

$$b\,\Delta Y = sY + dY = (s+d)Y, \tag{1.2}$$

dividing which through by Y and rearranging give a 10 per cent rate of growth (G):

$$G = \frac{\Delta Y}{Y} = \frac{s+d}{b} = \frac{.15+.1}{2.5} = .1 \tag{1.3}$$

Equation (1.3) implies a 25 per cent investment ratio, since

$$b\frac{\Delta Y}{Y} = \frac{I}{\Delta Y}\,\frac{\Delta Y}{Y} = \frac{I}{Y} \text{or } 2.5 \times .1 = .25 \tag{1.4}$$

The investment ratio given by (1.4) is what must be equated to the credit-creating economy's total 'savings' *including* long-term credit:

$$\frac{I}{Y} = \frac{S}{Y} + \frac{\bar{D}}{Y} \text{ or } bG = s+d;\ .25 = .15 + .1, \tag{1.5}$$

which is the condition for what Sir Roy Harrod calls 'progressive equilibrium', albeit in an explicitly credit-creating setting.[1]

In the light of such financial arrangements in Japan as described by equations (1.1)—(1.5), it is not at all surprising that Shimomura should make a seemingly paradoxical reference to Japan's 'rate of (capital) accumulation remaining very high despite her rising consumption level'.[2] If, therefore, greater investment can thus be financed partly by credits, there is no need for that 'abstinence' which the classical economists considered necessary for economic progress any more than there is for that 'austerity' which some present-day underdeveloped economies attempt to impose on already underconsuming populations at the constant peril of social unrest. Nor is it difficult, in such credit-creating circumstances, to agree with Keynes that consumption and investment should be considered *complementary* rather than competitive.[3]

MULTISECTORAL LINEAR PROGRAMMING

The macro model of credit-supported growth described by equations (1.2)

[1] See his *Towards a Dynamic Economics*, 1948.

[2] Shimomura, *op. cit.*

[3] '. . . capital is not a self-subsistent entity existing apart from consumption. On the contrary, every weakening in the propensity to consume regarded as a permanent habit must weaken the demand for capital as well as the demand for consumption.' (J. M. Keynes, *General Theory*, p. 106.)

—(1.5) can be reformulated in *multisectoral* terms,[1] and according to the standard *linear programming* technique of optimization used in Chapter 5.

Let the structural parameters (or pre-assigned policy parameters) of the i-th sector be

$$(2.1)\quad \begin{cases} b_{ji}=I_{ji}/\Delta Y_i, & (i, j=1,\ldots,n) \\ s_i=S_i/Y_i, & (i=1,\ldots,n) \\ d_i=\bar{D}_i/Y_i, & (i=1,\ldots,n) \\ \lambda_i=\Delta g/\Delta g_i. & (i=1,\ldots,n) \end{cases}$$

Here b_{ji} is the sectoral capital coefficient relating the additional capital-output of the j-th sector used by the i-th sector for capacity expansion, s_i the saving ratio in sector *i*, d_i the ratio of autonomous net borrowing (specifically for *investment* purposes) to output in sector *i*, and λ_i the valuation coefficient as before (albeit, $i=1,\ldots,n$ here, instead of $i=1,\ldots,4$). The parameters specified by (2.1) are nothing but the multi-sectoral equivalents of those specified by (1.1), though (2.1) includes λ_i which we discussed in Chapter 5 (esp. p. 57).

Next, let the *matrix* counterparts of (2.1) *for the whole economy* be given by

$$(2.2)\quad \begin{cases} B=\text{diagonal } (b_{ji}), \\ S=\text{diagonal } (s_i), \\ D=\text{diagonal } (d_i), \\ \Lambda=\text{diagonal } (\lambda_i). \end{cases}$$

Given the advance information specified by (2.1) and (2.2), we may formulate our optimization problem in matrix notation, thus:

Maximize the linear objective function

$$(2.3)\quad \varphi(G;\Lambda)=\sum_{j=1}^{n} \lambda_i g_i$$

in G (=diagonal (g_i)) subject to the linear constraints

$$(2.4)\quad BG \leqq \bar{S}+\bar{D},$$

and

$$(2.5)\quad G \geqq O,\ g_i \geqq O \text{ for all } i. \qquad (i=1,\ldots,n)$$

In this linear programming model, for a given set of λ_i's there is a unique combination of g_i's which will maximize and optimize G for the whole economy. Our optimization problem here is one of finding such values of *n* unknowns (g_i's) as would maximize the objective function (2.3) while meeting the constraints specified by (2.4) and (2.5). As in Chapter 5, *n* linear inequalities expressed by (2.4) must be replaced by *n* equations (via non-negative slack variables) in order to find *n* unknowns and hence a determinate solution. The maximand as well as optimand

[1] This multisectoral approach makes use of the input-output methodology initiated by W. W. Leontief, The *Structure of American Economy, 1919–1929—An Empirical Application of Equilibrium Analysis*, 1953. However, we shall neglect the static input-output transactions on current account and so concentrate on the dynamic net capital-formation aspect of a multisectoral economy.

G so determined would represent the best path of multisectoral growth, for it would mean that each sector is expanding its capacity by increasing its stock of capital up to the limit set by the available maximal supply of savings ($\overline{S}$) plus what maximal autonomous net borrowing ($\overline{D}$) makes possible, as the resource constraints (2.4) indicate in terms of ratios and in matrix notation.

It is to be stressed that the explicit *inclusion* of positive net intersectoral borrowing ($\overline{D} > O$) in this model (on the assumption of there being idle resources that could not be mobilized and utilized except by making capital funds available) enables each sector to contribute to overall optimal growth *better than* a usual savings-investment valance (as in a non-credit using model) would. Furthermore, if we regard D as including domestic *and* foreign net borrowing (for investment purposes), our linear programming model described by (2.1)—(2.5) again exemplifies the spirit of Keynes as well as the spirit of Schumpeter.

CHAPTER 6

THE 'TAKEOFF' PATH OF AN UNDERDEVELOPED ECONOMY*

Professor W. W. Rostow's idea of 'the takeoff into self sustained growth'[1] has attracted wide attention. However, favourable reactions to that idea have been mainly on the *ideological* ground that it has the effect of discouraging underdeveloped economies from emulating the rapid growth of authoritarian economies, while unfavourable reactions have been largely on the *historical-statistical* ground that the chronology of the takeoff attributed to the specific countries is disputable. These reactions seem to reflect a fundamental weakness in Rostow's historical approach to the takeoff, namely: historians' common tendency to draw an analogy between a past event and a present phenomenon in order to project it into the future as if history had to repeat itself instead of being moulded by man within wide limits and according to rapidly changing circumstances. Such a tendency merely strengthens the smug and superficial inference that, because it took some existing industrial societies half a century or more to take off into the mature stage of 'self-sustained growth', therefore the present-day underdeveloped societies should not aspire to a shorter transition—presumably except at the risk of impairing democratic institutions and human values.

I should like in this article to provide a *technical* justification of the understandably avid and hopeful feelings of present-day underdeveloped economies that they might, *through conscious public policy*, be able to take off into smooth stratospheric, if not supersonic, cruising—without dilly-dallying on the runway as long as some largely *laissez-faire* societies did in the past.

I. THE MECHANISM OF THE PROGRAMMED TAKEOFF

To elucidate the *economic* (in contradistinction to Rostow's historical) concept and mechanism of the takeoff, it is expedient to programme

* This originally appeared under the title of 'Dynamic Growth Programming for the "Takeoff" Path', *Indian Journal of Economics*, Vol. 41, No. 160, 1961.

[1] See Rostow, *The Process of Economic Growth*, 1952; 'The Take-Off into Self-Sustained Growth', *Economic Journal*, March 1956; and *The Stages of Economic Growth: A Non-Communist Manifesto*, 1960.

the long-range growth of an underdeveloped economy over a given programming horizon (say, fifteen years). Abstracting from the government and foreign-trade sectors in the interest of fundamental analysis, I suggest the following basic programming model in simplifying terms of *annual average* rates of change:

$$(1)\qquad Y^p_t=\rho_t N_t, \qquad (t=0, 1, 2, \ldots, n)$$

$$(2)\qquad \rho_{t+1}=\rho_t(1+\tau),$$

$$(3)\qquad N_{t+1}=N_t(1+\nu),$$

$$(4)\qquad Y^p_{t+1}=Y^p_t(1+g^p),$$

and so approximately

$$(5)\qquad g^p=\frac{Y^p_{t+1}}{Y^p_t}-1=(1+\tau)(1+\nu)-1=\tau+\nu,$$

$$(6)\qquad K_{t+1}-K_t\equiv I_{t+1}=b_{t+1}(Y^a_{t+1}-Y^a_t), \qquad (b_{t+1}-b_t<0)$$

$$(7)\qquad S_{t+1}=s_{t+1}Y^a_{t+1}, \qquad (s_{t+1}-s_t>0)$$

$$(8)\qquad b_{t+1}=b_t(1-\eta),$$

$$(9)\qquad s_{t+1}=s_t(1+\sigma),$$

$$(10)\qquad b_t(1-\eta)(Y^a_{t+1}-Y^a_t)=s_t(1+\sigma)Y^a_{t+1},$$

$$(11)\qquad g^a\equiv\frac{Y^a_{t+1}-Y^a_t}{Y^a_{t+1}}=\frac{s_t(1+\sigma)}{b_t(1-\eta)},$$

implying that

$$(12)\qquad \frac{I(t+1)}{\Delta Y^a(t+1)}\,\frac{\Delta Y^a(t+1)}{Y^a(t+1)}\equiv\frac{I(t+1)}{Y^a(t+1)}=\frac{S(t+1)}{Y^a(t+1)}.$$

$$(13)\qquad g^a=g^p \text{ or } \frac{s_t(1+\sigma)}{b_t(1-\eta)}=\tau+\nu$$

subject to the constraints

$$\frac{g^a}{\nu}>1 \text{ so that } \tau>0 \text{ or } \frac{d(\log Y^a)}{d(\log N)}>1 \text{ so that } \frac{d(\log \rho)}{dt}>0.$$

In this system of equations (1)–(13), the subscripts $t+1$ and t are respectively the next year (considered as an annual target year) and the base year of a, say, fifteen-year growth programme ($t=0, 1, 2, \ldots, 14$); Y^p is *potential full-employment output* (or desirable net real national income), Y^a *actual full-capacity output* (or feasible net real national income), N an employable labour population (= labour-input in full employment demanded *ex hypothesi*), K real capital when fully utilized, I net investment ($I_{t+1}=K_{t+1}-K_t$ on the assumption that $K_{t+1}=K_t+I_{t+1}$), and S net savings; g^p is the rate of growth of potential full-employment output, g^a the rate of growth of actual full-capacity output, ρ the average productivity or labour (or, to be specific, full-employment output per man-hour worked), b the investment coefficient (or the reciprocal of investment productivity), s the saving ratio, τ the rate of change in labour productivity, ν the rate of change in employable labour population, η the rate of change in the investment coefficient, and σ the rate of change in the saving ratio.

Equations (1)–(5) describe the normative aspect of growth programming in that they indicate how an ideal target rate of growth of output can be estimated by reference to the material needs and aspirations of a growing population with an increasing productivity. Thus equation (5) shows that if an underdeveloped economy's employable population increased by the constant percentage ν and if its labour productivity also increased by the constant percentage τ, its potential full-employment rate of growth would equal $\tau+\nu+\tau\nu$ or approximately $\tau+\nu$ (omitting $\tau\nu$ as a negligible order). I christened such a rate as given by (5) 'the socially optimal rate'.[1]

Equations (6)–(11), on the other hand, prescribe the parametric adjustments necessary to make actual output grow as fast as the potential output desired. To be specific, equations (6) and (7) express the dynamic functional forms of investment and savings based on the assumption that the coefficients involved change from the base year t to the next year $t+1$. Equation (8) specifies the dynamic investment coefficient as capable of *decreasing* by the constant percentage η from period t to period $t+1$ on the policy assumption that it can and must be decreased (or, in other words, investment productivity $1/b$ can and must be increased). Likewise, equation (9) specifies the dynamic saving ratio as capable of *increasing* by the constant percentage σ from period t to period $t+1$ on the policy assumption that the average propensity to save can and must be increased. The specific implementation of these parametric assumptions will be suggested in the next section.

Equation (10) states the saving-investment equilibrium condition to be satisfied for the following target year $t+1$ if actual output is to be maintained or if the existing stock of capital is to be fully utilized. Equation (11), which results from equation (10), gives us the annual average rate of growth of actual full-capacity output. It implies that the investment ratio equals the saving ratio at $t+1$, as equation (12) clearly indicates. Finally, equation (13) furnishes the dynamic mechanism of the takeoff, provided that the elasticity of actual full-capacity output is *greater than unity* with respect to employable labour so that the rate of growth of labour productivity may be *positive* (since $g^a/\nu \equiv (\Delta Y^a/Y^a)/(\Delta N/N)$ and $\tau \equiv \Delta\rho/\rho$). We may illustrate the implications of equation (13), as follows:

If $g^a-\nu<0$, then $\tau<0$. (pre-pre-takeoff path)
If $g^a-\nu=0$, then $\tau=0$. (pre-takeoff path)
If $g^a-\nu>0$, then $\tau>0$. (*takeoff* path)

[1] See my *The Keynesian Theory of Economic Development*, 1959, pp. 44 ff.

Since the rate of growth of labour productivity is a good first approximation to the rate of growth of *per capita* real income, a positive τ signifies a rising standard of living over the programming horizon. Thus viewed, the underdeveloped economies in pre-takeoff conditions are characterized by a stationary standard of living (expressed in $\tau=0$), owing to the unitary elasticity of actual output with respect to employable labour (expressed in $g^a-\nu=0$). It follows, therefore, that those underdeveloped economies aspiring to take off into sustainable growth with a rising standard of living would have to meet, at least, the takeoff requirements specified by equation (13).

II. RELEVANT POLICY IMPLICATIONS

The practical question now is: how does an underdeveloped economy go about influencing the key variables *b* and *s* so as to change them in the desired directions? Specifically, it is necessary to indicate that the investment coefficient can be *decreased* (or investment productivity increased) and the saving ratio *increased* between the base year *t* and the target year t+n in order to justify the policy assumptions

$$(8') \qquad \frac{b_{t+n}}{b_t}=(1-\eta)^{t+n-1} \text{ or } \frac{b_{t+1}}{b_t}=1-\eta, (t=0, 1, 2, \ldots, n)$$

and

$$(9') \qquad \frac{s_{t+n}}{s_t}=(1+\sigma)^{t+n-1} \text{ or } \frac{s_{t+1}}{s_t}= 1+\sigma. (t=0, 1, 2, \ldots, n)$$

A complete answer to the above question would involve such far-reaching changes in human nature, social institutions and economic organization as are clearly beyond the purview of the present technical undertaking. Nevertheless it seems useful to emerge with a partial answer in the light of the peculiarities of an underdeveloped economy, and in an operationally meaningful manner.

Policywise, it is helpful to think of the investment coefficient as a function of two strategic variables:

$$(14) \qquad b=\frac{I}{\Delta Y}=\frac{\Delta K}{\Delta Y}=\frac{K}{Y}=\frac{K}{N}\frac{N}{Y}=\frac{K/N}{Y/N},$$

where K/Y is the capital-output ratio (=ΔK/ΔY on the assumption of a linear homogeneous two-factor production function), K/N the capital-labour ratio, N/Y the labour-output ratio, and Y/N labour productivity. Equation (14) reveals *b* as capable of changing directly with the capital-labour ratio (K/N) and inversely with labour productivity (Y/N). To assume, therefore, that the investment coefficient can and must be decreased from the base year *t* to the target year t+n or, alternatively, from the base year *t* to the next year $t+1$ as (8′) indicate is to imply that labour productivity should be increased in greater proportion than the capital-labour ratio, or $\Delta(Y/N)/(Y/N) > \Delta(K/N)/(K/N)$, *as a matter of deliberate policy*. In other words, the productivity function of the form $Y/N = F(K/N)$ shifts upward, implying that labour productivity (Y/N) is greater for the same combination of capital and labour (K/N=const.)—even though the numerator K may be quantitatively significant relative to the denominator N at any instant of time during the capital-requiring phase of industrialization.

Such an upward shift of the productivity function is the essence of J. A. Schumpeter's dynamic concept of 'innovation' involving an entirely new higher level of productive know-how instead of a merely different combination of K and N in a given state of know-how.[1] Mrs Joan Robinson also seems to favour such a dynamic shift of the productivity function as a possible alternative to the Ricardo effect (profit-wage relation serving as a market mechanism to adjust any discrepancy between the rate of growth of capital and the rate of growth of population), especially if imperfect competition or institutional rigidities prevents the smooth operation of the market mechanism.[2] A deliberate policy to increase labour productivity faster than the capital-labour ratio, furthermore, is perfectly consistent with the quest of the whole population for a secularly rising standard of living (expressed in a positive τ in equation (13)).

Turning now to the saving ratio (s), how can an underdeveloped economy implement the policy assumption expressed by (9′) *supra*? The classical notion of promotion thriftiness via greater income inequality is both impractical and superfluous in the context of a present-day underdeveloped economy, especially if such an economy represents also a welfare state. For greater income *equality* rather than inequality would be found more conducive to increasing s from period *t* to period $t+n$ or, more simply, to period $t+1$, quite contrary to the classical assumption. However, it is necessary to specify greater income equality as a result of a deliberate policy to redistribute (via fiscal and other measures) income from the rentier group (especially absentee landlords and usurers) with an observably small marginal propensity to save to the entrepreneur group with an observably large marginal propensity to save. Such a result can in turn lead to a larger saving ratio for the whole economy, as follows:

[1] See Schumpeter, *The Theory of Economic Development*, 1934.

[2] See J. Robinson, *The Accumulation of Capital*, 1956. Also see my interpretation of the Robinsonian growth model in *The Keynesian Theory of Economic Development*, pp. 73–80.

Let there be the income identity of the form

$$(15)\qquad Y \equiv W + Q + R,$$

where Y is net real national income (= Y^a), W wage-income, Q profit-income, and R rent-income (including pure interest). Then the distribution ratios follow from (15):

$$(16)\qquad \frac{W}{Y} = \alpha,\ \frac{Q}{Y} = \beta,\ \frac{R}{Y} = 1 - \alpha - \beta.$$

Next, let the saving identity take the form

$$(17)\qquad S \equiv S_w + S_q + S_r,$$

the right-hand side of which can be specified as

$$(18)\qquad S_w = s_w W, \qquad (s_w = 0)$$

$$(19)\qquad S_q = s_q Q, \qquad (s_q > 0)$$

and

$$(20)\qquad S_r = s_r R. \qquad (s_r < s_q > 0)$$

Here we assume that the marginal (= average, as in long-run saving functions with zero intercepts) propensity to save out of wage income (s_w) equals zero and that the marginal propensity to save out of profit-income is not only positive but also larger than that out of rent-income ($s_q > s_r > 0$). These assumptions seem plausible to make for most underdeveloped societies where the rentier is addicted to 'conspicuous consumption', and where the bulk of wage-earners save nothing or dissave most of the time.

Then identity (17) can be rewritten

$$(21)\quad S \equiv s_w \alpha Y + s_q \beta Y + s_r (1 - \alpha - \beta) Y = [s_w \alpha + s_q \beta + s_r (1 - \alpha - \beta)] Y,$$

from which we obtain the saving ratio for the whole economy when $s_w = 0$:

$$(22)\qquad s \equiv \frac{S}{Y} = s_q \alpha + s_r (1 - \alpha - \beta),$$

which clearly indicates the possibility of the saving ratio increasing as a result of a rise in the profit-income distribution ratio (β) at the expense of an equal fall in the rent-income distribution ratio ($1 - \alpha - \beta$) —without at all lowering the wage-distribution ratio (α) which is likely to be already low relative to the former two ratios, especially in the context of an underdeveloped economy characterized by extreme income disparities.

Thus it is, not an inter-redistribution from wage-income to property-income, but an *intra*-redistribution from one kind of property income (i.e. functionless rent-income including usury) to another (i.e. functional profit-income) that seems justified both economically and socially in an underdeveloped economy with an inordinately redundant group of rentiers. Thus 'the euthanasia of the rentier' advocated by Keynes in the context of an advanced economy and in favour the entrepreneur seems to apply *a fortiori* to an underdeveloped economy.[1] In addition, the rentiers' perverse capital exports (to advanced economies) and attempts to keep up with the international Joneses would also have to be restrained through appropriate exchange and import controls in the specific case of an open system with foreign-trade relations. Needless to say, a more comprehensive growth programme would include capital imports and budget surpluses as supplementary means of increasing s.

If an underdeveloped economy could thus be programmed so as to take off into sustained growth more quickly than under *laissez-faire*, it, far from impairing democratic values, would on the contrary thereby strengthen those values. For the more rapidly and permanently are poverty, unemployment, ignorance and other characteristic ills of an underdeveloped economy cured by conscious public policy, the less fertile will be the soil on which authoritarian ideas and practices could thrive and the more solid will be the material basis for forwarding spiritual values.

[1] *General Theory*, p. 376.

CHAPTER 7

MIXED ECONOMIC STATECRAFT AND DEMOCRATIC SAFEGUARDS*

The less developed economies bent upon rapid growth are understandably tempted to adopt the extreme form of centralized economic planning. especially in these times of hyper-susceptibility to the international 'demonstration effect' (the higher consumption and production standards of advanced economies). To resist such a temptation is not to discourage the idea of economic planning but to encourage the *democratic* pattern of growth programming in the *long-run* interest of the developing economies concerned. This essay is broadly intended to be an additional contribution to the literature on the state role in economic development. To be more specific, this essay will discuss the rationale, operational significance, and practical applicability of mixed economic statecraft most closely associated with the name of Keynes, and also suggest the necessary safeguards against the possible abuses of that statecraft in any developing economy that might be inclined to adopt it.

I. KEYNESIAN MIXED STATECRAFT

The anonymity and impersonality of the modern 'mixed economy',[1] so-called, is in itself a great scientific advance over the emotion-laden labels 'capitalism' and 'socialism'. However, since the concept of a mixed economy represents an ingenious combination of the advantages of capitalism and socialism without their disadvantages, it seems useful to begin with an introductory discussion of the disadvantages of extreme statecraft.

On the one side, there is a policy of *laissez-faire* designed to leave individual economic decisions and activities entirely unchecked even when those activities lead to general instability, insecurity and inequity. Here economic man is assumed to be so rational, economic

* Originally appeared under the same title in *Social and Economic Studies* (published by the Institute of Social and Economic Research, University College of the West Indies, Jamaica), June 1961.

[1] As far as I am aware, Professor A. H. Hansen was the first to coin this expression. See his *Fiscal Policy and Business Cycle* (W. W. Norton, N.Y.), 1941.

calculus so precise, economic machinery so efficient, and private property so sacrosanct that inferentially almost nothing and nobody should be subjected to public control. Here is the one extreme case of statecraft where individual liberty is misconstrued as individual licence, where political democracy is undermined by economic anarchy, where private virtues are mistaken for the public good, and where private initiative is misinterpreted as a sufficient as well as necessary condition for economic and social progress. The only notable exception to this rule has been the public control of 'big business' in the interest of greater atomistic competition. Even today there are a few economists and policy-makers who are interested and concur in the government's function *only* as 'the preserver of competition' on the classical assumption that competition is an 'all-sufficient' regulator, stabilizer and innovator.

On the other side, there is a policy of authoritarian planning aimed at organizing individual economic units into 'classes' for central control at the calculated risks of class wars, partisan strife, personal hatred, and individual injustice. Here central authority is assumed to be so omnipotent, economic man so class-conscious, personal choice so antisocial, and public ownership so indispensable that, by implication, almost everything and everybody should be subjected to public control. Here is the other extreme case of statecraft where economic planning is abused by political totalitarianism, where the national interest is misrepresented by class interests, and where public policy is misinterpreted as the self-sufficing, self-justifying promoter of all economic blessings, social and personal. The only promising exception to this rule is seen in the avowed attempts of some existing authoritarian regimes to 'decentralize', presumably in the interests of economic efficiency, individual initiative and consumer choice. Even outside those regimes there are a few economists and policy-makers who contemplate and manipulate the agencies of the state for the authoritarian or autocratic control of economic life on the dogmatic assumption that complete regimentation is the only alternative to complete *laissez-faire*.

It was as offering a better alternative to those extreme types of statecraft that Keynes conceived his *mixed* statecraft, with a specific view to providing technical means to three technical ends, namely: (*a*) full and stable employment; (*b*) greater equality in the distribution of wealth and income in so far as it would aid the first aim; and (*c*) the international homogenization of living standards, especially in the postwar period of reconstruction and development. These are, it is to be stressed, essentially *technical* ends, since their attainment requires rigorous analysis, dispassionate judgment, and clear perception, irrespective of what political attitude or ideological bearing the social scientist may have. Obviously these goals are so great in magnitude and so global in scope that they can be reached only with the aid of the state possessing sufficient resources and the power to use them in the public interest. These technical objects become political issues when they are deemed inconsistent with non-economic goals of society or when they are reached by emotional means. However, apprehensions about the political danger of achieving 'full employment at any cost', intimations about the political instability of 'an egalitarian society', insinuations about 'the road to serfdom', and other misgivings about the consequences of Keynesian statecraft will be found unwarranted when seen in the clear light of Keynes's own democratic premise and technical precaution.[1]

To see the practical usefulness of Keynesian mixed statecraft more readily, it is only necessary to recall the following advantages, as compared with the disadvantages of extreme statecraft indicated above:

First, Keynesian analysis and policy would leave individual economic units perfectly free to pursue their self-interest, thus letting producers maximize their profits, consumers maximize their utility, savers maximize their security or amenity, investors maximize their marginal efficiency of capital, etc. In other words, microeconomic units do not constitute subjects of Keynesian statecraft. Thus the principles of free enterprise, competitive pricing, consumer sovereignty and private initiative are left intact.

Second, macroeconomic aggregates, such as total saving, total consumption and total investment, constitute the subjects of Keynesian public control, and they cut across economic classes. As such, these aggregates have the effect of declassing 'the working class', 'the capitalist class' and other emotion-ridden labels. For instance, the Keynesian concept of 'the propensity to save', which is a variable subject to public control, does not admit of blame on any one class when it misbehaves relatively to the given inducement to invest so as to reduce effective demand (in the short run) or to retard economic growth (in the long run).[2] For the propensity to save is an impersonal macroeconomic variable which incorporates

[1] Keynes, while advocating a 'system of State Socialism' to exercise 'a guiding influence' on private economic decisions and activities, nevertheless was careful to add such qualifications as 'the common will, embodied in the policy of the State' and 'whilst preserving efficiency and freedom'. (See the concluding chapter in the *General Theory*.)

[2] To be more precise, saving can be said to misbehave in the sense that it falls short of full-employment investment to create an inflationary gap or exceeds full-employment investment to create a deflationary gap—according to the familiar short-run income mechanism of the form $\Delta Y = f\ (I - S)$, where ΔY is

the saving propensities of individuals and groups of individuals, regardless of what 'class' they may represent from a sociological or ideological point of view. The same holds valid for all other macroeconomic variables which are to be made subject to public control in a Keynesian mixed economy; these variables simply do not lend themselves to the fanning of emotions.

Third, macroeconomic variables subject to Keynesian public control are operationally significant in the sense that they are measurable as definite quantities and quantitative relations, thus making scientific control and prediction possible within technical limits. The technical limits here refer to the dynamic nature of human behaviour, the variability of socio-cultural data impinging on economic man's decisions and activities, and the logical necessity of making the simplifying assumptions of constant behaviour patterns for useful prediction. These limits are, of course, characteristic of all *social* sciences. The main point to be stressed here is that the subjects of Keynesian public control permit quantitative manipulation and plausible prediction, thereby lending themselves readily to scientific analysis and objective policy.

Fourth, and lastly, the variables subject to Keynesian public control are related to national income and wealth in such a way as to allow *indirect* monetary and fiscal control mechanisms to operate effectively, thus rendering direct controls (e.g. rationing, priority allocations, price fixing, and import quotas) largely superfluous. For monetary and fiscal policies are capable of influencing the behaviour of saving, consumption, investment, and other macroeconomic variables through their influence on national income and wealth. Moreover, the effective use of monetary and fiscal policies would make the doctrinaire espousal of public ownership irrelevant. This does not, however, imply that Keynesian statecraft dogmatically excludes direct controls or public ownership under all circumstances, for surely experience warrants the complementary use of direct controls and supplementary resort to public ownership under some circumstances (e.g. wartime, underdeveloped economies without much private initiative and capital,[1] trading nations with persistent

an increment (or a decrement) of effective demand, I investment, and S savings. In the long run, on the other hand, it is as causing an inflationary or deflationary divergence from the equilibrium rate of growth that saving can be said to misbehave—when that equilibrium rate is given by $\Delta Y'/Y'=s/b$, where Y' is productive capacity, s the average propensity to save out of full-employment real income, and b the average and marginal capital-output ratio. (For detail see my *The Keynesian Theory of Economic Development*, London, 1959.)

[1] Cf. R. J. Alexander, 'State vs. Private Enterprise in Latin America', *American Journal of Economics and Sociology*, January 1958.

balance-of-payments difficulties, and advanced economies with strong democratic safeguards).

II. DEMOCRATIC SAFEGUARDS AGAINST ABUSES

The democratic principle was so much of a second nature to Keynes[1] that he apparently considered it redundant to specify democratic safeguards against the possible abuses of central authority in the economic field. None the less, his digressive remarks here and there are helpful in enumerating the kinds of safeguards which a mixed economy ought to evolve, as follows:

1. The central controls necessary to guide the smooth functioning of a mixed economy should be coupled with a public policy of encouraging 'the decentralization of decisions and of individual responsibility'.[2] Such a policy implies a due diversification of central authority at the national, provincial and local levels, collaboration between the public and private sectors, and the co-functioning of the price mechanism and the public-control mechanisms. To the extent that these implications are brought out as a matter of deliberate policy, to that extent will democratic values (e.g. the exercise of personal choice, the variety of life, the love of the common man, and the independence of mind) be helped rather than hindered. To that extent, conversely, totalitarian homogeneity and authoritarian inelasticity will be averted.

2. The necessary central controls should be supplemented by a public policy of fostering the natural evolution of public-spirited, public-relations-conscious, semi-autonomous private enterprises and institutions (e.g. public utilities, banks, schools and churches) as well as of constructing built-in stabilizers and equalizers (e.g. social security programmes, progressive taxation, collective-bargaining legislation, fair-employment-practice legislation, and public housing and schooling). Such a policy would help safeguard a mixed 'welfare state' against the abuses of collectivism inasmuch as the need for complete planning and the clamour of sentimental egalitarianism would thereby be mitigated.

3. The necessary central controls should be implemented by the creation and protection of autonomous monetary and fiscal agencies free from partisan political considerations and private lobbies, that is, government agencies armed with permanent control powers as well as with flexible control mechanisms—subject to the ultimate Parliamentary constraint. Here the traditional principle of monetary sovereignty protecting the independence of central bank policy-making

[1] See R. F. Harrod, *The Life of John Maynard Keynes* (N.Y., 1951).

[2] *General Theory*, p. 380.

must be extended to a fiscal authority entrusted with the task of applying fiscal measures in the interests of economic stability and growth.

4. The state should encourage 'the collection and dissemination on a great scale of data relating to the business situation, including the full publicity, by law if necessary, of all business facts which it is useful to know'.[1] Such a policy of promoting mass enlightenment on economic affairs would make for more effective democratic voting[2] and policy-making, while at the same time making against demagogic pleading. Mass education is therefore a powerful long-run safeguard against theoretically unsound policy-making in the economic field as well as in other fields.

5. The state should be willing to 'entrust to science the direction of those matters which are properly the concern of science'.[3] Applied to economic policy-making, this would mean that the economic problems of national and international importance should be discussed, analysed and approached for their solution in the spirit of 'Bretton Woods' (monetary conferences of international experts at Bretton Woods, NH, USA). Apropos, Sir Roy Harrod tells us that 'Keynes tended till the end to think of the really important decisions being reached by a small group of intelligent people, like the group that fashioned the Bretton Woods plan'.[4] He then raises the pertinent question: 'But would not a democratic government having a wide multiplicity of duties tend to get out of control and act in a way of which the intelligent would not approve?'[5] Neither Keynes nor Harrod answers this question, however. One might answer that the possible danger of a democratic government resorting to undemocratic solutions to economic problems is likely to be lessened by its executive branch working closely with its legislative and judiciary branches, as a truly democratic government should, as well as by its policy-makers having the benefit of the vision and precaution of technical advisers in and out of the government service.[6]

[1] Keynes, *Essays in Persuasion* (London, 1952), p. 318.

[2] An enlightened voting public is presupposed by C. A. R. Crosland when he asserts: 'Any Government which tampered seriously with the basic structure of the full-employment Welfare State would meet with a sharp reverse at the polls; and this knowledge acts as rather a strong inducement to politicians not to tamper.' (See his *The Future of Socialism*, London, 1957, p. 61.)

[3] Keynes, *Persuasion*, p. 373.

[4] See his *The Life of John Maynard Keynes*, p. 193.

[5] *Ibid.*

[6] It is fitting, in this regard, to cite Keynes's own defence of experts: 'I dare to speak for the much abused so-called experts. I even venture sometimes to prefer them, without intending any disrespect, to politicians. The common love of truth, bred of a scientific habit of mind, is the closest of bonds between the representatives of divers nations.' (Speech on the International Monetary Fund before the House of Lords, May 23, 1944.)

CHAPTER 8

ACHIEVING AND DIFFUSING ECONOMIC AFFLUENCE*

Mankind has come a long way from the day when economic scarcity was regarded as an immutable law of nature, and when the sheer struggle for subsistence was the common concern of people everywhere. Indeed, until relatively recently we had been taught to look upon poverty, unemployment and underconsumption as unfortunate but unavoidable. For it was not until the appearance of Keynes's *General Theory* that 'the paradox of poverty in the midst of plenty' was explained in a way that left no doubt in the minds at least of economists that a potentially wealthy society *need not* allow itself to become actually poor enough to save only as much as can be offset by *laissez-faire* investment.[1] Having initiated the historic shift from the classical 'economics of scarcity' to the modern 'economics of potential plenty', as D. Dillard aptly describes,[2] Keynes went further to envisage a much wider diffusion of economic abundance than was thought possible or desirable by most of his contemporaries.

My purpose in this essay is to explore *macro political-economic* ways and means of achieving and diffusing affluence—beyond the technical confines of growth economics[3] and distribution theory, and from the vantage point of post-Keynesian thinking. Such an exploration may be found particularly relevant to underdeveloped economies that are trying to achieve a measure of affluence both absolutely and in relation to what K. Galbraith has chosen to call 'the affluent society'.[4]

I. ACHIEVING ECONOMIC AFFLUENCE

For the majority of nations and individuals in the real world the

* Originally appeared in *Indian Economic Journal*, July 1960.

[1] *General Theory*, pp. 30–1.

[2] See Dillard, 'The Influence of Keynesian Economics on Contemporary Thought', *American Economic Review*, May 1957.

[3] For more narrowly technical ways and means, see my *The Keynesian Theory of Economic Development* (London, 1959).

[4] See Galbraith's book of the same title, Boston, 1958. There he discusses the nature and survival of the American economy with its rising general productivity and mass purchasing power, albeit critically as well as glowingly. He does not discuss the international homogenization of affluence, however.

primary problem is one of achieving a measure of affluence, although diffusing economic affluence will become more and more urgent as time goes on. It seems, therefore, useful to amplify Keynes's view of the fundamental factors governing 'the *pace* at which we can reach our destination of economic bliss',[1] as follows:

1. The rapid growth of population has hitherto been welcome as expanding market demand or military manpower, but henceforth population growth will have to be adjusted to capital growth for maximum *per capita* income and continuous full employment while giving greater emphasis to eugenics subsequently. The community's basic choice between work and leisure governing the size of a labour force will be altered increasingly in favour of leisure as population growth is better adjusted quantitatively and qualitatively to the other conditions of economic progress. Here economics, sociology, technology, medical science and family ethics would all have to join in a concerted effort to manage man's propensity to procreate as rationally as educated families in any quarter of the civilized world are already doing today.

2. That the warless state of human affairs is a social as well as economic desideratum is easy to see, but its realization calls for far more political wisdom and moral courage than nations and individuals seem to possess at present. The milieu of a lasting peace is necessary for expanding trade throughout the world, for greater confidence in the future, for maximum private initiative and risk-taking, and for avoiding unproductive investment in armaments as well as preventing the wasteful destruction of the existing capital stock—in sum, for a closer approximation to the promised land of abundance. At the present juncture of human history Sweden and Switzerland are rare instances of a peaceful democratic society that enjoy high living standards and great cultural advantages by deliberately avoiding any involvement in international and civil wars. Keynes's earlier criticism of 'the narrow scientific vision of the professional soldiers', diplomats' 'inelasticity of mind', and politicians' lack of 'imaginations'[2] and 'international idealism' as militating against world peace is applicable *a fortiori* to the present period of a restless peace that exists in the shadow of nuclear war.

3. Above all, it is the ceaseless unfolding and outpouring of technological know-how that is most likely to carry all of us with it into the lap of unprecedented opulence. For technology is man's ultimate answer to the challenge of niggardly Nature. Already taking place

[1] See his 'Economic Possibilities for our Grandchildren' (1930), reproduced in *Essays in Persuasion* (London, 1952), p. 373.

[2] See his *Essays in Biography* (N.Y., 1951), esp. Part 1.

before our bewildered eyes and to our astounded ears are the sight and sound of commercial jet-flying, atomic-powered plants, outer-space rockets, intercontinental missiles, and flying jeeps. The wonder is, however, less for the exciting promise all these marvellous devices hold out to economic man than for the terrifying implications of their destructive application for all mankind. It is encouraging, though, to hope that men of science responsible for the conquest of space and time will some day place their common obligation to humanity above their narrow dedication to technicality, for international conferences of scientific experts are already proving the didactic significance of Keynes's observation: 'The common love of truth, bred of a scientific habit of mind, is the closest of bonds between the representatives of divers nations.'[1]

4. Closely allied to technological advance is the accumulation of capital.[2] Fundamentally capital is accumulated or decumulated, depending on whether the community consumes less or more than it produces after allowing for depreciation, that is, on there being positive or negative net savings in real terms. Keynes, while he unorthodoxically stressed the deflationary danger of excessive saving relative to investment in the short run, nevertheless essentially concurred with classical economists in the long-run importance of net saving for the growth of productive capacity, albeit differing from them in not leaving it to private decisions alone. It is no accident, therefore, that modern growth theories of the operationally significant type are of the Keynesian origin. Nor is it any wonder that the capital-rich members of the world family should enjoy material affluence absolutely and in relation to its capital-poor members. Capital accumulation is not, as some writers have it, an alternative to technological advance in the development of capital-scarce countries. Rather, capital accumulation should be looked upon as an indispensable *complement* to technological advance in mankind's march toward the promised land of opulence. Thus there is much wisdom in already capital-rich, technologically-advanced nations becoming even more capital-rich, technologically-advanced so as to benefit capital-poor, technologically-backward nations, by repercussion.

It is one thing to shift from potential to actual affluence by meeting the fundamental prerequisites of economic progress outlined above, but it is quite another to diffuse actual affluence, once achieved,

[1] Speech before the House of Lords, May 23, 1944.

[2] Cf. Joan Robinson, *The Accumulation of Capital* (Homewood, 1956); R. Nurkse, *Problems of Capital Formation in Underdeveloped Countries* (Oxford, 1953).

among as many nations and individuals as possible. For, as Keynes observed, 'the critical difference' will be realized when the experience of abundance becomes 'so general that the nature of one's duty to one's neighbour is changed'.[1] How to make economic affluence so *general* as to render economic scarcity *passe* and good life a common lot remains to be pondered. This is where we must turn to the second primary task of diffusing economic abundance.

II. DIFFUSING ECONOMIC AFFLUENCE

The utilitarian principle of 'the greatest happiness of the greatest number' serves as a democratic basis for a social policy of effecting a wider diffusion of material abundance, both nationally and internationally.

We begin at the national level first. So that economic affluence may become as general as Keynes envisaged, it is necessary for a nation to build into its economic structure and social fabric more *stabilizers* and *equalizers* than at present. Otherwise economic affluence would remain an ephemeral and sectional state of affairs even if nations and individuals succeed in meeting the basic prerequisites of rapid growth, and even if mankind enjoys greater affluence today than in the past. Ephemeral because economic affluence would diminish or vanish if the economy as a whole allowed itself to have more and longer slumps than booms, on balance. Sectional because economic affluence would remain the privilege of a few individuals or groups of individuals if society allowed itself to perpetuate the undemocratic principle of hereditary property and the monopolistic concentration of wealth and income.

We have learned from men like Keynes and Lord Beveridge to evolve a host of built-in stabilizers and equalizers within the general framework of a mixed public-private economy and a democratic welfare-state society, and without resort to totalitarian tyranny and egalitarian monotony. Thus in Western democracies we already have such built-in stabilizers as full-employment legislation, social-security plans, ready-made public-works programmes, permanent or flexible fiscal-monetary compensatory mechanisms, and farm-price support schemes. Thus in those democracies we already have also such built-in equalizers as progressive taxation, anti-monopoly legislation, minimum-wage laws, fair-employment practice laws, public-school systems, public-housing programmes, mass production, and mass communications. To be sure, some of those stabilizers and equalizers

[1] *Persuasion*, p. 372.

technically overlap or contradict each other,[1] but it is the principles of those things that have far-reaching implications. To the extent that the stability of income, employment and general prices and the equality of opportunity become *faits accomplis*, to that extent will economic affluence be the common lot of people. So the *mixed public-private economy* and the *democratic welfare-state society* are a helpful pair of spectacles with which we can catch a glimpse of the promised land of diffused abundance.

Turning now to the international level, the utilitarian diffusion of economic affluence would have to include an attempt to homogenize the quantitatively divers living standards of nations,[2] if *general* abundance is to become *truly* general. For both experience and idealism tell us that it is economically unsound and politically unwise to perpetuate a world divided into a few 'have' nations and a great many 'have-not' nations. Economically unsound because extreme living-standard disparities militate against both the rapid growth of underdeveloped economies for lack of capital and the stable growth of advanced economies for lack of demand. Here what need to be harmonized are the productivity aspect of saving relevant to the long-run growth of underdeveloped economies and its non-spending, demand-aspect pertinent to the shorter-run stability of advanced economies. Politically unwise because the existence of a wide living-standard gap between 'have' and 'have-not' nations tends to induce the former to 'divide and rule' while at the same time tempting the latter to raise the general living standard quickly even at the expense of personal liberty and private initiative. Here what need to be harmonized are the understandable impatience of 'young' poor nations and the demonstrable tolerance of 'old' rich nations.

The reader will, in this respect, recall Keynes's serious concern with, and great contribution to, the postwar problem of narrowing international living-standard gaps to the mutual benefit of developed and underdeveloped nations. Also, J. Tinbergen, in boldly recommending a world policy to harmonize and homogenize the rates of growth of real national incomes per head, reminds us that 'there is an ever increasing gap between the real incomes of the wealthiest and the poorest areas'—a gap which he regards as 'probably the most alarming divergency'.[3] Thus it would seem that the diffusion

[1] Compare my 'Professor Hansen on America's Economic Revolution', *Economic Journal*, September 1958.

[2] This problem will receive further and greater attention in the next Part of this volume on 'International Prosperity and Progress'.

[3] See his 'An International Economic Policy', *Indian Journal of Economics*, July 1957.

of affluence misses much of its broad appeal if it is not extended to the global scene so as to help the backward areas to advance economically and in other ways.

The wider diffusion of affluence on the national and international fronts can hardly be entrusted to the traditional principle of 'functional distribution' alone; it involves a deliberate political decision based on broader principles. A modern combination of Adam Smith's 'political economy', John Stuart Mill's 'utilitarian' ethics and the historic 'egalitarianism' of social reformers would be needed here to reinforce the social philosophy of Keynes aimed at a future as well as present-day free and affluent society.

PART III

INTERNATIONAL PROSPERITY AND PROGRESS

CHAPTER 9

THE INTERNATIONAL COMPATIBILITY OF GROWTH AND TRADE*

Traditional writers have been anxious to show that the postwar drive to narrow the standard-of-living gap between underdeveloped and developed nations would also narrow the scope for the operation of the classical principle of comparative advantage and hence contract rather than expand exports from developed nations.[1] The purpose of this note is to demonstrate a theoretical possibility of underdeveloped economies rapidly growing relatively to advanced economies to the benefit of the export trade of advanced economies[2]—quite contrary to prevailing growth-trade pessimism.

For pedagogic convenience we may make the simplifying assumption that the world economy is made of the developed sector and the underdeveloped sector, each sector representing a homogeneous unit. We shall thus abstract from the intra-sectoral trade so as to concentrate on the inter-sectoral. In addition, let us take relative prices and exchange-rates as given so that we may isolate the dynamic influence of relative *income movements* on world trade. The relevant conceptual difference between the developed sector and the underdeveloped sector will then be found to lie in the idiosyncratic manners

* Originally published in *Economia Internazionale*, August 1960.

[1] For such traditional views see J. Viner, *International Trade and Economic Development*, 1952; J. H. Williams, *Trade Not Aid: A Program for World Stability*, 1953; J. R. Hicks, 'An Inaugural Lecture', *Oxford Economic Papers*, June 1953; Committee for Economic Development, *National Objectives and the Balance of Payments Problem*, February 1960. A notable exception will be found in H. G. Johnson, 'Increasing Productivity, Income-Price Trends and the Trade Balance', *Economic Journal*, September 1954.

[2] It is interesting, in this connection, to recall Keynes's optimistic foresight: 'But as soon as possible, and with increasing emphasis as time goes on, there is a second primary duty laid upon it (the proposed World Bank for Reconstruction and Development), namely, to develop the resources and productive capacity of the world, with special attention to the less developed countries, to raising the standard of life and the conditions of labour everywhere, to make the resources of the world more fully available to all mankind, and so to order its operations as to promote and maintain equilibrium in the international balances of payments of all member countries.' (Opening Remarks at the First Meeting of the Second Commission on the World Bank, July 3, 1944; printed in *The New Economics*, S. E. Harris, ed., 1948, Chap. 29, p. 397.)

in which those sectors grow domestically and trade internationally. We shall presently specify and quantify the idiosyncracies involved. So much for the general background. Let us proceed with the building of a two-sector model of growth and trade to illustrate the main argument.

As far as the advanced sector is isolatedly concerned, insufficient effective demand is the ultimate bottleneck to its rate of growth of output.[1] For no matter how great its supply potential might be, the advanced sector's actual growth would be technically limited to the extent to which prevailing effective demand would permit. Accordingly we shall assume that the domestic growth of the advanced sector as a whole is uniquely determined by the technical relation of investment-demand and saving. Solving the familiar income-expenditure equation of the form $Y_a=(1-s')Y_a+\bar{I}$ (where Y_a is the advanced sector's real net national income demanded or simply effective demand, $\bar{I}$ autonomous investment-demand, and s' the marginal propensity to save) for ΔY_a, we get the domestically determined rate of growth of effective demand for the advanced sector in isolation:

$$\text{(1)} \qquad \left(\frac{\Delta Y}{Y}\right)_a=\frac{i}{s'},$$

where $i=\Delta\bar{I}/Y_a$ or the advanced sector's ratio of additional autonomous investment-demand to the effective demand. Equation (1) shows the rate of growth of effective demand in the advanced sector as capable of varying directly with the ratio of additional autonomous investment-demand to real income and inversely with the marginal saving ratio. As such, equation (1) is nothing but the dynamic version of Keynes's multiplier theory (since $\Delta Y_a=1/s'(\Delta\bar{I})=\Delta\bar{I}/s'$ in comparative-statistics, where $1/s'$ is the multiplier coefficient for the closed system).

Now the advanced sector considered as an 'open' system has a certain elasticity of demand for imports from the underdeveloped sector with respect to domestic income, that is:

$$\text{(2)} \qquad \eta_a=\left(\frac{\Delta M}{M}\right)_a\bigg/\left(\frac{\Delta Y}{Y}\right)_a,$$

where η_a is the trend value of the advanced sector's income elasticity of demand for imports from the underdeveloped sector, $(\Delta M/M)_a$ and $(\Delta Y/Y)_a$ being respectively the rate of change in real imports and the rate of change in real income. What (2) expresses is the degree to which the advanced sector growing at the rate given by (1)

[1] The 'advanced' sector here is, *ex hypothesi*, confined to market economies.

secularly responds as an importer of goods and services produced in the underdeveloped sector. The elasticity coefficient (η_a) reflects the advanced sector's tastes for foreign-produced goods, the import-contents of its domestic-produced goods (including the exportable), the nature of its import function, its tariff schemes, and other structural factors. Empirical evidence seems to justify the hypothesis that the income elasticity of demand for consumer goods and agricultural produce in world markets is generally smaller than that of capital goods and manufactures.[1] This implies that the advanced sector's income elasticity of demand for imports from the underdeveloped sector tends to be less than unity as a rule and on the whole ($\eta_a < 1$), though the demand for specific imports may exhibit far greater or less sensitivity with respect to income change. Moreover, the longer is the period in view, the greater will be the quantitative significance of the structural changes mentioned above and the greater also will be the income elasticity of demand for imports in world markets.

From (1) and (2) we have the advanced sector's rate of growth of imports in the functional form

$$(3) \qquad \left(\frac{\Delta M}{M}\right)_a = \eta_a \frac{i}{s'},$$

which indicates that the advanced sector's real imports can grow at a rate equal to the income elasticity of demand for imports (η_a) times the rate of growth of effective demand (i/s′). It is this rate of growth of imports which must be brought into equality with the given rate of growth of exports, if there is to be equilibrium in the advanced sector's trade *vis-a-vis* the underdeveloped sector. This is where we have to turn to the underdeveloped sector's growth of imports which constitutes the advanced sector's growth of exports, since

$$(4) \qquad \left(\frac{\Delta X}{X}\right)_a \equiv \left(\frac{\Delta M}{M}\right)_u,$$

where $(\Delta X/X)_a$ is the advanced sector's rate of growth of exports and $(\Delta M/M)_u$ the underdeveloped sector's rate of growth of imports. Identity (4) expresses the basic truism that one nation's imports represent another nation's exports, and *vice versa.* But then the undeveloped sector's rate of growth of imports must be determined independently and in relation to its own growth of income.

As far as the underdeveloped sector is domestically concerned, insufficient capital is the ultimate bottleneck to its rate of growth of output. For however great its demand potential might be, the underdeveloped sector could not grow faster than its actual capital accumulation would permit. Thus it is plausible to assume that the domestic

[1] Cf. T. C. Chang, *Cyclical Movements in the Balance of Payments*, 1951.

growth of the underdeveloped sector as a whole is uniquely determined by the quantity and quality of capital. Making use of the familiar Harrod-Domar growth equation, we have for the underdeveloped sector in isolation:

$$(5) \qquad \left(\frac{\Delta Y'}{Y'}\right)_u = \sigma s,$$

where $(\Delta Y'/Y')_u$ is the underdeveloped sector's rate of growth of output,[1] σ the average or marginal productivity of capital in full use (representing the quality of capital), and s the average saving ratio (representing the quantity of capital). It is this rate of growth of output given by (5) which largely determines the underdeveloped sector's growth of imports, the exact extent of that latter growth depending on the trend value of its income elasticity of demand for imports given by

$$(6) \qquad \eta_u = \left(\frac{\Delta M}{M}\right)_u \Big/ \left(\frac{\Delta Y'}{Y'}\right)_u.$$

The elasticity coefficient (η_u) given by (6) depends on the structural factors mentioned in connection with the advanced sector's counterpart (η_a). Inasmuch as imports into the underdeveloped sector consist largely of capital goods and manufactures, it may be presumed that the trend value of η_u generally exceeds unity, by far. Furthermore, it seems plausible to assume that the underdeveloped sector's income elasticity of demand for imports from the advanced sector rises secularly in the course of its industrialization requiring greater and greater imports of capital goods. This assumption will be found important presently.

From (5) and (6) we have the underdeveloped sector's rate of growth of imports:

$$(7) \qquad \left(\frac{\Delta M}{M}\right)_u = \eta_u \sigma s$$

which reveals that the underdeveloped sector's real imports are capable of growing in direct proportion to the income elasticity of demand for imports (η_u) times the productivity of capital (σ) times the saving ratio (s). It is this rate of growth of imports into the underdeveloped sector which constitutes the advanced sector's rate of growth of exports, as stated earlier. Accordingly we can express the condition of external equilibrium to be satisfied by the advanced sector in the form

[1] We arrive at this rate of growth from $Y'=\sigma K$, $\Delta Y'=\sigma\Delta K$, $\Delta K=I$, and $I=S$, where Y' is real net national income supplied or simply productive capacity, K real capital, I net investment, and S net savings. For detail see my *The Keynesian Theory of Economic Development*, 1959, pp. 62 ff.

$$(8)\qquad \left[\left(\frac{\Delta M}{M}\right)_u \equiv \left(\frac{\Delta X}{X}\right)_a\right] - \left(\frac{\Delta M}{M}\right)_a = 0 \text{ or } \eta_u \sigma s - \eta_a \frac{i}{s'} = 0.$$

There is, of course, no reason to suppose that the equilibrium condition specified by (8) will be automatically established, for both the trend values of import-demand elasticity and the rates of growth of income associated with the two types of economy, advanced and underdeveloped, cannot be equal except by accident. But what is more interesting to know is whether the advanced sector's rate of growth of exports (or, what amounts to the same, the underdeveloped sector's rate of growth of imports) is likely to be faster or slower than its rate of growth of imports in the course of global economic development. For this purpose it seems useful to exemplify equation (8) by putting $G_a = (\Delta Y/Y)_a$ and $G_u = (\Delta Y'/Y')_u$ and holding G_a and η_a constant, as in Table 1:

TABLE 1

Structural Parametric Relations Assumed	*Rate of Growth of Exports from the Advanced Sector*				*Rate of Growth of Imports into the Advanced Sector*		
	η_u	$G_u \equiv$	$\left(\frac{\Delta X}{X}\right)_a$	$\gtrless$	$\left(\frac{\Delta M}{M}\right)_a$	$= \eta_a$	$\cdot\ G_a$
$\eta_u = \eta_a$, $G_u < G_a$	1	.02	.02	<	.05	1	.05
$\eta_u > \eta_a$, $G_u < G_a$	1.5	.04	.06	>	.05	1	.05
$\eta_u > \eta_a$, $G_u < G_a$	2	.06	.12	>	.05	1	.05

We may interpret Table 1 thus: Generally speaking, if the income elasticity of demand for imports is the same for both sectors ($\eta_u = \eta_a$), as in the first row, the world's trade balance depends, *cet. par.*, on the relative rates of growth of real income. Thus if the advanced sector's rate of growth exceeds that of the underdeveloped sector ($G_a > G_u$), as in the first row again, the former's rate of growth of exports is below its rate of growth of imports. But in the heterogenous nature of global economic development the underdeveloped sector's income elasticity of demand for imports can show an upward secular trend, as in the second and third rows, thus reflecting its increasing needs for manufacturers in general and capital goods in particular. If so, the rapid growth of the underdeveloped sector's real income may well give rise to the secularly rising rate of growth of imports or of exports from the advanced sector, as the second and third rows indicate. This does not imply that any particular advanced economy's balance of trade can thus improve secularly, since the income elasticity of demand for imports differs from one commodity to another and since the rate of growth of income also differs from one trading nation to another.

Nevertheless our analysis leads us to the conclusion that the rapid growth of real income in the underdeveloped areas of the world, while it might entail the loss of comparative advantage on the part of some advanced economies, all the same could expand imports to their own benefit and thereby help expand exports from advanced economies as a whole—in a manner exemplified by Table 1 above.

CHAPTER 10

THE AGENDA FOR INTERNATIONAL EQUILIBRIUM*

My specific purpose in this essay is twofold, to wit: (*a*) to explore possible foundations for international amity in the light of Keynesian economics, and (*b*) to extrapolate Keynesian internationalism in a policy-making, problem-solving manner. Such an essay may also throw useful light on the great issue of war and peace in our nuclear age.

I. THE ECONOMIC MILIEU FOR WORLD PEACE

It is important to explore possible economic foundations for international amity, not because international strife is caused by the economic factor alone, but because the creation of an amicable and viable economic *milieu* is an indispensable preliminary to durable world tranquillity, stability and equity. Let us do so in the light of Keynesian internationalism.[1]

Universalization of Full Employment. Simultaneous realization and maintenance of full employment throughout the world is one of the most important technical conditions for international amity, for two reasons. First, a full-employment world would be largely spared the struggle for markets characterized by 'beggar-my-neighbour' expedients, autarchy, and other discriminatory practices making for international enmity. For 'if nations can learn to provide themselves with full employment by their domestic policy . . . there would no longer be a pressing motive why one country need force its wares on another or repulse the offerings of its neighbour', as Keynes put it.[2]

* Originally published under the title of 'An Extrapolation of Keynesian Internationalism', *Economic Studies Quarterly*, March 1961.

[1] For Keynes's early efforts in the cause of world peace, see *The Economic Consequences of the Peace* (1920), and also Harrod's comments in the chapter of the same title (VII) in *The Life of John Maynard Keynes*. For Keynes' own vivid personal account, see 'Dr. Melchoir: A Defeated Enemy', in *Two Memoirs* (1949). For Keynes's influence on international economics and policies see *The New Economics* (S. E. Harris, ed.), especially Part 5 entitled 'International Economic Relations'.

[2] *General Theory*, p. 382.

Thus full employment must not, as was done by classical economists, be simply assumed but must, as Keynes taught, be *realized* if international trade is to cease to be 'a desperate expedient to maintain employment at home by forcing sales on foreign markets and restricting purchases',[1] and also if the struggle for markets is to cease to be a causal factor in war.

This first reason carries with it an international obligation for principal trading nations to maintain full and stable employment by their domestic policy, for small changes in their income and hence imports cause so great fluctuations in the income and employment of the rest of the world as to necessitate all sorts of self-protective measures that merely worsen international economic and political relations.[2]

The second of these reasons, one which Keynes anticipated but did not elaborate, is that a full-employment world, especially in an age of 'power politics', would be spared an otherwise inevitable tendency to make an ideological-political issue out of what is essentially a technical problem. For the absence of mass unemployment in some areas of the world and its presence in other areas are conducive to exaggerated claims for the economic beauty of a planned full-employment society on the one side and equally exaggerated counterclaims for the non-economic value of an unplanned *laissez-faire* society on the other side, both sides thus trying to influence the 'uncommitted' nations on the ideological-political front. There is no gainsaying that full employment, however achieved and maintained, would provide some nations with an enormous propaganda advantage over other nations who, for the fear of inflation or for the love of *laissez-faire*, are more rather than less inclined to tolerate mass unemployment. For the majority of so-called small nations in the actual world are plagued with persistent mass unemployment (though for reasons more directly related to the next topic—economic backwardness) and hence are willing to experiment with desperate expedients for full employment, regardless of ideological implications. Few would deny that mass unemployment, wherever and whenever used as a weapon of ideological warfare, tends to heighten rather than diminish the world's tension.

The second reason carries with it an international obligation for great powers to maintain full employment[3] within their national

[1] *General Theory*, pp. 382–3.

[2] Cf. *The Business Cycle in the Post-War World* (E. Lundberg, ed.), London, 1955.

[3] Apropos, the so-called 'Keynes Plan' (for an International Clearing Union) states: 'If active employment and ample purchasing power can be sustained in the main centres of world trade, the problem of surpluses and unwanted exports will largely disappear.' (*Ibid.*, IV (18).)

borders as well as to help maintain it in smaller nations in order to prevent, among other things, dictators and demagogues, 'to whom war offers, in expectation at least, a pleasurable excitement', from inflaming 'the natural bellicosity of their people'.[1] For experience shows that ordinary people everywhere are more prone to be bellicose toward the foreigners made out to be the scapegoats when they are troubled by domestic mass unemployment and depression than when they are not.

A promising start in the direction of universal full-employment consciousness was made by the United Nations' *National and International Measures for Full Employment*,[2] both the authorship (especially N. Kaldor and A. Smithies) and the substance of which unmistakably reflect an impact of Keynesian thinking. A more practical step was seen in the establishment of the International Monetary Fund which Keynes helped to blueprint, and one specified purpose of which is 'to contribute thereby to the promotion and maintenance of high levels of employment and real income' (Agreement Article I (i)). There would have to be a sharper functional division of labour and a less confused state of policy-making, if the International Monetary Fund and the International Bank for Reconstruction and Development are to attend to cyclical unemployment and structural underemployment respectively,[3] instead of pretending to possess a 'catch-all' remedy for those distinct and different types of unemployment, however.

Homogenization of Living Standards. Another major economic precondition of international amity is the homogenization of living standards among nations. For so long as the world is sharply and conspicuously divided into 'haves' enjoying high living standards and 'have-nots' enduring low living standards, so long will its 'have-not' members remain covetous, suspicious and rebellious and its 'have' members cautious, ostentatious and imperious—all to the great detriment of international goodwill and placidity. In no other area is the imaginative application of Keynes's macroeconomic approach and his global prescience needed more urgently and greatly. Let us proceed to outline such an application.

First, Keynes's saving-investment theory designed for a 'closed'

[1] *General Theory*, p. 381.

[2] Lake Success, N.Y., December 1949. See also my 'The United Nations and Full Employment', *Journal of Political Economy*, August 1950.

[3] For the conceptual difference between these two types of unemployment, see my *The Keynesian Theory of Economic Development* (Chapter 6), London, 1959. Joan Robinson has called those types 'Keynesian unemployment' and 'Marxian unemployment' respectively. (See her 'Marx and Keynes', in *Collected Economic Papers*, London, 1951.)

system can be broadened to include the world economy as a whole, as Keynes himself suggested. To Keynes, the world's homogenization of living standards was an essentially technical question of making the saving propensities of its capital-rich members compatible with the investing propensities of its capital-poor members.[1] For if the real income of a nation is shown capable of rising as a result of domestic saving-investment interaction on a larger scale, the real income of the whole world can also be shown capable of growing as a consequence of greater international saving-investment activity, to the mutual benefit of capital-exporting nations with high saving propensities and capital-importing nations with high investing propensities.[2] Thus dynamized in an international setting, Keynes' saving-investment theory could be a powerful tool for analysing and directing (*a*) the growth of *per capita* real income of the world as a whole, (*b*) the rapid economic development of underdeveloped countries, and (*c*) the stable growth of advanced economies.[3]

Second, Keynes's recommendation that the then proposed World Bank 'develop the resources and productive capacity of . . . the less developed countries'[4] must be applied in a *wider* context including *all* capital-rich and capital-poor nations regardless of ideological or political differences, if the financing of economic development on a global scale is to be truly multinational and technical in nature. A failure to bring some capital-rich nations into membership of the existing World Bank would merely encourage and perpetuate a present tendency to extend financial and technical assistance to capital-poor nations on a unilateral and politico-military basis. Alas, competitive lending by power-conscious, ideology-minded nations outside and beyond the framework of the World Bank is bound to increase rather than decrease international tension, even though the economic growth of underdeveloped countries is accelerated as a by-product of such lending. So important a long-run matter as the development of backward economies should not be left to the accident of myopic ideological warfare or capricious power-politics any more than it should be left to the chance of *laissez-faire* capital movements. This is the lesson implicit in Keynes's proposals for international financial instruments on 'a purely technical and non-political basis'.[5]

In line with Keynes's notion of international economic homo-

[1] See *The Keynes Plan*, IX (5).

[2] Cf. R. F. Harrod, *Dynamic Economics* (esp. pp. 106–15); C. Clark, 'The World Will Save Money in the 1950's', *Fortune*, July 1950.

[3] In this respect, see my 'The International Compatibility of Growth and Trade', *Economia Internazionale*, August 1960.

[4] Speech before the World Bank Commission, July 8, 1944.

[5] *The Keynes Plan*, 1 (f.).

genization, the United Nations called attention to the paramount importance of devising practical 'Measures for the Development of Under-developed Countries'[1] expressly with an immediate view to narrowing the existing living-standard gaps, and undoubtedly with an ultimate view to fostering international amity, by repercussion. The World Bank, which is the brain child of Keynes, has played a quantitatively significant role in the postwar financing of less developed economies. However, the World Bank would have to make its technique applicable on a *more* 'technical and non-political' basis as Keynes intended, if it is to facilitate the truly multinational meeting of capital-rich and capital-poor nations to their mutual advantage.

Third and last, Keynes's proposal for the national control of population can be approached from an *international* point of view. Viewing 'the pressure of population' as one of the 'economic causes of war',[2] Keynes suggested that nations learn to 'attain equilibrium in the trend of their population'.[3] Regarding population also as one of the governing factors of economic progress, he proposed that we exercise 'our power to control population' in order to realize 'economic possibilities for our grandchildren'.[4] In addition, Keynes advocated eugenics as the basic for a possible *qualitative* control of population, for he suggested: 'The time may arrive a little later when the community as a whole must pay attention to the innate quality as well as to the mere number of its future members.'[5] Apparently he thought of the control of population, both as a possible cause of war and as a potential factor of economic progress, primarily in terms of a national policy. But the time has come when the control of population can be effected on an international basis and in the interests of world peace and world progress, judging from the activities and interests of the World Population Conference.

II. THE AGENDA FOR A FUTURE DEMOCRACY OF NATIONS

We now turn to the broader and far-reaching implications of Keynesian internationalism. Two major wars have been fought to make the world 'safe for democracy'. And yet the postwar world is still ablaze with impetuous nationalism, explosive anti-colonialism, militant neutralism, hostile insularism, aggressive anti-foreignism,

[1] See the publication of the same title, N.Y., May 1951, and also my 'The United Nations and Economic Development', *Indian Economic Journal*, April 1954.

[2] *General Theory*, p. 381.

[3] *Ibid.*, p. 382.

[4] *Essays in Persuasion* (London, 1952), p. 373.

[5] *Ibid.*, p. 319.

and offensive racialism. Indeed it is hard to imagine a world of greater tensions and frictions or of greater ill will and mutual distrust among nations. Nevertheless, it would be a tragic error to draw pessimistic or cynical conclusions from the superficial observation of the surface events, however disturbing and exasperating. For if the world has in the past greatly profited by Adam Smith's global concern with 'the wealth of nations', it surely can in the future learn a great deal from Keynes's hopeful vision of a 'new democracy of nations'.[1]

Keynes's vision of a future democracy of nations was based on his optimistic convictions that 'the solidarity of man is not a fiction', that 'nations can still afford to treat other nations as fellow-creatures' and that 'the prosperity and happiness of one country promotes that of others'.[2] What he perceptively characterized as the essence of international power-politics after World War I is all too applicable to the contemporary state of affairs after World War II, namely: that mankind or a large part of it is torn between 'the obligations of humanity' and 'the fear of Bolshevism'.[3] Such a state of international affairs seems to call for some bold re-examination. We suggest the following agenda as worthy of Keynesian internationalism:

1. *An international agreement to outlaw war as an instrument of national policy, with appropriate sanctions against violating nations.* Such an agreement is in keeping with Keynes's view that 'our determination to avoid wars and civil dissensions' is a fundamental prerequisite of human progress.[4] It is also in accord with his pleading: 'On Peace Questions let us be Pacifist to the utmost.'[5] The promulgation of such a legal prohibition of war by itself might not prevent future wars, but it would greatly reinforce the academic argument for world peace. In this respect, General Douglas MacArthur may have broken fresh ground by incorporating into the new constitution of defeated Japan the renouncement of war as an instrument of national policy. The basic difficulty with the MacArthur scheme, though, appears to lie in its unilateral character, apart from the retrospective fact that 'the fear of Bolshevism' led to its virtual breakdown in Japan as it led to the reversal of the initial policy in disarmed Germany. All the same, the MacArthur scheme for postwar Japan does point to a possibly wider application.

[1] Speech, House of Lords, May 18, 1943.

[2] *Persuasion*, p. 29.

[3] See his 'Dr. Melchoir', in *Two Memoirs*.

[4] *Persuasion*, p. 373.

[5] *Ibid.*, p. 330. See also Elizabeth Johnson, 'Keynes's Attitude to Compulsory Military Service', *Economic Journal*, March 1960.

2. *An international agreement on the limitation of armaments.* This agendum is more urgent in the present age of potential nuclear-missile warfare than when Keynes declared himself 'in favour of giving a very good example . . . in the direction of Arbitration and of Disarmament'.[1] The United Nations' Disarmament Commission is already moving slowly but hopefully in the direction of universal disarmament—under the increasing pressure from those member nations who are most likely to fall innocent victims to any future nuclear-missile war.[2] It is significant that Bertrand Russell, who shared with Keynes the distinction of being considered Alfred Whitehead's two best pupils at Cambridge, should have found it necessary to write his *Common Sense and Nuclear Warfare*.[3] Russell, like Keynes, seems to imply that nations ought to rely more on their moral strength and less on their military might for permanent defence and peace—on the premise that all future international disputes can and must be settled through moral suasion and collective wisdom. The oftheard complaint of 'neutralist' countries that 'nations talk of peace and prepare for war'[4] must not be dismissed wholly as idealistic or unrealistic, for the outcome of an unrestrained armament race among the nuclear powers could well mean co-expiration, as Bertrand Russell and other thoughtful scientists have knowledgeably warned.

3. *An international guarantee of the self-determination of purely internal affairs.* Keynes applied the principle of self-determination in his proposal for an International Clearing Union when he stated: 'There should be the least possible interference with internal policies. . . . The technique of the plan must be capable of application, irrespective of the type and principles of government and policy existing in the prospective member States.'[5] This implies that nations ought to be left free to solve their own social and political problems by their own methods without extraneous interference, except when such national policies obviously endanger world peace. Indeed, the word 'freedom' seems to small nations to mean primarily freedom from all forms of foreign interference, just as it seems to poor nations to mean primarily freedom from hunger. An international guarantee of the principle of self-determination would go a long way toward eliminating unnecessary charges and countercharges of

[1] *Persuasion*, p. 331.

[2] Noteworthy is such a world conference as was sponsored by the Japanese Committee for the Prevention of Atomic and Hydrogen Bombs (August 1958).

[3] Simon & Schuster, N.Y., 1959.

[4] See, e.g., S. L. Parmar, 'Future of World Trade'. *Indian Journal of Economics*, July 1957.

[5] *The Keynes Plan* (preamble).

'colonialism' and uneasy unilateral attempts at 'neutralism' as a measure of self-protection.

4. *An international policy of fostering the social and racial equality of nations.* The implied approval of such a policy can be inferred from Keynes's basic regard for 'freedoms of persons, of thought, and faith', his well-known friendship toward people of divers racial and cultural origin, his subtle rebuke of 'anti-Semitism', his support of the feminist movement, and his marriage to a Russian ballerina. The rationale of such a policy is easy to see in the light of the historical experience that so much international friction was caused by the doctrine of 'white man's burden', the myth of 'Aryan supremacy', and such other pretexts to 'civilize' so-called backward peoples. It is also easy to see in the light of the anachronistic fact that great social inequalities persist in many tradition-bound areas of the world, to provoke such bitter and cynical resentment against aristocracy, plutocracy, authority, masculinity, the elite, and the caste system as to produce grave international repercussions. The United Nations' commissions on human rights, women's status and refugees are promising steps in the right direction, but much more needs to be done if nations are to live and work as equal 'fellow-creatures' in a true democracy of nations.

Such are the agenda for a 'saner, kinder world', as Keynes envisaged.[1] The United Nations, with all its youthful weaknesses, nevertheless seems to be the best available instrumentality for discussing and implementing such agenda as well as for establishing the economic foundations for world amity discussed in the preceding section. The democracy of nations will be the crowning achievement of posterity, signifying the ultimate triumph of international reason over national passions, of the cosmopolitant outlook over the insular bias, of humanity over sovereignty, of peace over war. The international ideas and ideals of Keynes have already made and will continue to make a great contribution to that achievement.

[1] See King's College, *John Maynard Keynes, 1883–1946*, p. 9.

CHAPTER 11

TOWARDS A WORLD ECONOMIC GOVERNMENT*

If nations were once willing to sacrifice part of their sovereignty in the interest of international equilibrium even at the expense of domestic equilibrium during the gold-standard age, might they not work towards the establishment of 'the future economic government of the world', as the British White Paper hopefully suggested in connection with *The Keynes Plan* (for an International Clearing Union)? Having destroyed the gold standard almost single-handedly, Keynes undertook the task of constructing a new regulator of international economic conduct, with a view to facilitating multilateral trade and 'guiding a distressed and confused world into the ways of peace and economic order'.[1] He made a distinctive contribution to international trade thinking by introducing two new basic principles,[2] namely: (*a*) that there must be 'a central institution, of purely technical and non-political character, to aid and support other international institutions concerned with the planning and regulation of the world's economic life',[3] and (*b*) that there must be international currency and trade systems which 'combine the advantages of a freedom of commerce with safeguards against the disastrous consequences of a *laissez-faire* system which pays no direct regard to the preservation of equilibrium and merely relies on the eventual working out of blind forces'.[4] The International Monetary Fund may be considered a first approximation to Keynes's ideal of a world economic government, but further requirements alongside the accomplishments must be pointed out, as follows:

* Originally published in *Panjab University Economist* (Pakistan), October 1959.

[1] Speech, House of Lords, December 18, 1945.

[2] Cf. J. Robinson, 'The International Currency Proposals', *Economic Journal*, June-September 1943; J. E. Meade, *Planning and the Price Mechanism*, Allen and Unwin, London, 1948 (esp. Chap. 5); R. Nurkse, 'Domestic and International Equilibrium', and R. Hinshaw, 'Keynesian Commercial Policy', in *The New Economics* (S. E. Harris, ed.); L. A. Metzler, 'The Theory of International Trade', in *A Survey of Contemporary Economics* (H. S. Ellis, ed.), Blakiston, Philadelphia, 1948.

[3] *The Keynes Plan*, I (f.).

[4] Speech, House of Lords, December 18, 1945.

(i) *Universal Currency Convertibility.* Keynes considered it a *sine qua non* of multilateral trade to make all national currencies freely convertible into one another rather than into gold and in terms of some super-national unit of account, so that 'the money earned by selling goods to one country can be spent on purchasing the products of any other country'.[1] At present gold and the dollar alone possess unequivocal universal acceptability, which is the essential quality of convertible international money, all other national currencies being partly or completely inconvertible for *current* payment purposes (currency inconvertibility for *capital* account purposes being sanctioned by the International Monetary Fund). If this incomplete currency convertibility is a by-product of what many nations still regard as 'a hostile world', then universal currency convertibility may well be a significant cause as well as an effect of an amicable world.[2]

(ii) *Flexible Exchange Stability.* Experience[3] led Keynes to propose a new regime of stable yet flexible exchange-rates.[4] Under such a

[1] Speech, House of Lords, May 18, 1943. Apropos, how objective and international Keynes was in his thinking can be seen in his statement criticizing 'little Englandism' and supporting multilateral finance: 'As a technique of little Englandism adopted as a last resort when all else has failed us, with this small country driven to autarchy, keeping itself to itself in a harsh and unfriendly world, it (a system of bilateral and barter agreements) might make sense. But those who talk this way . . . can have very little idea how this Empire has grown or by what means it can be sustained.' (His speech on the International Monetary Fund, House of Lords, May 23, 1944.)

[2] To clinch our understanding of the benefits of currency convertibility, it is only necessary to recall the disadvantages of the alternatives involved, namely: barter-like bilateral finances tending not only to hinder the international division of labour but also to distort trade into political channels, the difficulty or impossibility of a deficit nation paying a surplus nation by direct exports, instead of exporting to any part of the world and applying the proceeds to meet the obligations in the surplus country, and the absurd necessity of possessing or accumulating gold as the only generally convertible medium of international exchange.

[3] The historic gold standard with its exchange rigidity made it impossible for deficit nations to achieve external equilibrium except by deflating domestic prices, income and employment, that is, by passively accepting domestic disequilibrium. This was the main reason why Keynes so valiantly fought against the gold standard (see his 'The End of the Gold Standard', in *Persuasion*), and also why nations went off gold during the 'thirties. The regime of free exchange-rates which had replaced the gold-standard regime went to the other extreme of producing exchange anarchy, such that trading nations not only indulged in self-defeating 'exchange dumping' to gain temporary export advantages but lost confidence in the stability of money to the detriment of international trade and finance. The post-war establishment of the International Monetary Fund was intended to combine the advantages of the gold standard and the system of free exchange-rates without their disadvantages.

[4] Cf. his speech on International Monetary Fund, House of Lords, May 23, 1944.

new regime, a deficit nation would be free, within prescribed limits, to devalue its currency[1] to achieve external equilibrium without upsetting internal equilibrium, though whether the resulting low export price and high import price could actually stimulate exports and discourage imports to the desired extent depends on other factors as well.[2] It is also to be noted that a regime of stable yet flexible exchange-rates makes use of a *managed* price mechanism in the international field, instead of relying on the *laissez-faire* 'specie-flow-price mechanism'. However, there is, under the present International Monetary Fund arrangements, some confusion of exchange stability and exchange fixity, as in the past, owing to a dogmatic tendency never to alter the dollar price of gold under any circumstances.[3]

(iii) *Managed International Liquidity.* Keynes favoured the application of national central banking principles to the international field, so that all trading nations might have access to anonymous short-term credit facilities without suffering a 'run' in their foreign exchange reserves or without having to increase domestic unemployment for the sake of foreign payments equilibrium.[4] Such credit facilities, like the individual possession of liquid reserves, would 'allow time and method for necessary adjustments and a comfortable safeguard behind which the unforeseen and the unexpected can be faced with equanimity'.[5] An international pool of foreign exchange reserves should, in Keynes's view, be coupled with the permanent national control of foreign-exchange flows *on capital account* or, more specifically, with the permanent control of short-term capital

[1] The technique involved may be illustrated thus: A devaluing country simply raises the domestic price of gold, as Britain in 1949 raised the sterling price of gold per ounce from £8.7 to £12.5, thus lowering the external value of the pound sterling from about £.25=$1 to about £.35=$1 (or $4=£1 to $2.80=£1). Such a technique would have the effect of making exports cheaper in terms of undevalued foreign currencies and of making imports dearer in terms of the devalued national currency.

[2] E.g., the price-income elasticities of demand for imports and trend forces in operation.

[3] In this respect, see Harrod's criticism of such a tendency, in his *The Dollar*, Harcourt, N.Y., 1954.

[4] 'Where financial contributions are required for some purpose of general advantage, it is a great facility not to have to ask for specific contributions from any named country, but to depend rather on the anonymous and impersonal aid of the system as a whole. We have here a genuine organ of truly international government.' (*The Keynes Plan*, IX (40).)

[5] *The Keynes Plan*, IV (16). The 'necessary adjustments' involved here seem to refer to the time-consuming tasks of increasing productivity, discovering new markets, making structural improvements, and influencing international tastes.

movements of a speculative and disequilibrating nature.[1] The continued practices of unilateral short-term lending, bilateral financing, illicit exchange depreciation, extra-legal capital flight, involuntary interest-rate fluctuation, domestic deflation, and discriminatory protectionism are strongly indicative of the inadequacy, imperfection and incomprehensiveness of the existing international liquidity arrangements associated with the International Monetary Fund.

(iv) *Regulated Commercial Liberty*. In place of the *laissez-faire* policy of 'free trade', Keynes wanted to substitute a new policy of internationally-regulated commercial liberty, with due allowance for exceptional circumstances requiring trade restrictions as well as for 'national diversities of policies' (e.g. 'state-trading and bulk purchasing').[2] Thus he welcomed the proposed but not established International Trade Organization, having as its declared aims the multilateral reduction of tariffs, the conscious co-ordination of foreign-trade policy and domestic employment policy, and the reciprocal co-operation between surplus and deficit nations, between developed and underdeveloped countries,[3] and between primary-commodity producing and manufacturing economies. For he never 'supposed that in the final outcome the monetary proposals should stand by themselves'.[4] Despite the establishment of the General Agreement on Tariffs and Trade and other hopeful signs,[5] ideo-

[1] Keynes stressed two specific advantages of such an internationally-sanctioned capital control mechanism, namely: to enable trading nations to retain domestic control over their interest-rate policy and to prevent the perverse flight of capital from deficit to surplus countries 'for political reasons or to evade domestic taxation or in anticipation of the owner turning refugee.' (See his speech, House of Lords, May 23, 1944, and also *The Keynes Plan*, VII (32).) A third advantage might be added, that of preventing short-term capital flight from jeopardizing capital-poor countries' long-run aim of economic development.

[2] Speech on the Anglo-American Financial Arrangements, House of Lords, December 18, 1945, and also *The Keynes Plan*, VIII (37), entitled 'Relation of the Clearing Union to Commercial Policy'.

[3] Apropos, J. E. Meade states: 'The underdeveloped countries, moreover, can, for the purpose of promoting industrial development, be given limited exemptions from certain of the rules and procedures limiting protectionism. In return they can agree to co-operate with developed countries in the consideration and determination of what are really sensible and economic development projects.' (*Planning and the Price Mechanism*, pp. 111–12.) Similarly, a representative of an underdeveloped economy states: '. . . if restriction implied temporary contraction of trade in order to bring about future expansion, it becomes an auxiliary of the natural forces. That is why the infant industry argument from which commercial policy of many nations draws inspiration is accepted as just and fair by advocates of liberalism in international trade.' (S. L. Parmar, 'Future of World Trade', *Indian Journal of Economics*, July 1957.)

[4] Speech, House of Lords, May 23, 1944.

[5] Some of the hopeful signs are seen in the US Randal Commission Report of

logically-minded economic *blocs*, politically-oriented regionalism, politically-motivated unilateralism, militarily-dominated aid programmes, retaliatory protectionism, bilateral trade agreements and commodity-price disaccords continue to exist, thus calling forth greater international efforts to supplement the monetary and financial policies with regulated and enlightened commercial policies.

1954, the post-war discussion around the European Payments Union, and the more recent negotiations for a 'free-trade area' in Europe.

CHAPTER 12

TOWARDS A DEMOCRACY OF NATIONS*

I should like in this essay to bring out some far-reaching implications of Keynesian thinking for the intrinsically universal desiderata of narrower standard-of-living gaps, less ideological strife and more elastic political sovereignty, in sum, for a permanent 'democracy of nations'.[1] For such a purpose one would have to search for the broader and deeper aspects of Keynes than are found in the technical pages of the *General Theory*, and also to extend those aspects further, as I shall endeavour to do on this occasion.

Let us begin by pondering the future implications of the Keynesian observation: 'The political problem of mankind is to combine three things: Economic Efficiency, Social Justice, and Individual Liberty.'[2] In thus perceiving the fundamental problem of human society Keynes suggestively considered the goals of economic efficiency and individual liberty as requiring such 'technical knowledge' and 'appreciation of the excellencies of variety and independence' as had traditionally been associated with the Liberal Party, while viewing the goal of social justice as depending on such 'an unselfish and enthusiastic spirit which loves the ordinary man' as had historically been exemplified by the Labour Party.[3]

If nations could accept economic efficiency, social justice and individual liberty as their *common* goals, then the technical knowledge of advanced economies, the egalitarian spirit of welfare-States, and the libertarian traditions of free societies would all have to be co-ordinated in a non-partisan, multi-national manner, *especially in this day and age when no single nation or political party possesses the exclusive monopoly of technical know-how, public-welfare policy and civil liberties.* Here, then, is a powerful suggestion that assumes an air of practical urgency in a technologically narrowing yet ideo-

* Originally appeared under the same title in *Kautilya* (published by Mysore University, India), June 1962.

[1] The phrase is due to Keynes, in his speech on 'The International Clearing Union' before the House of Lords, May 18, 1943.

[2] Keynes, 'Liberalism and Labour', in *Essays in Persuasion*, pp. 344–5.

[3] *Ibid.*

logically widening world. Any person or nation taking such a suggestion at all seriously would surely refrain from making heat-generating ideological issues out of such technical problems as the unemployment and poverty of underdeveloped economies or out of such ethical problems as social justice and individual liberty. Instead, a person or nation would have to 'entrust to science the direction of those matters which are properly the concern of science' and to 'value ends above means and prefer the good to the useful' and so 'return to some of the most sure and certain principles of religion and traditional virtue', as Keynes perceptively forewarned.[1]

Let us, next, consider the interesting results and challenging implications of Keynes's long-run vision. It would be a serious error to infer a basic lack of time-perspective from Keynes's oft-quoted dictum that 'in the long run we are all dead'. For, contrary to the popular belief, Keynes never lost sight of time-perspective even in dealing with purely and seemingly short-run problems. This we know, not only because Keynes himself taught us to 'study the present in the light of the past for the purposes of the future',[2] but also because J. A. Schumpeter observantly ascribed to Keynes a propensity 'to implement an essentially long-run vision by a short-run model'.[2] Otherwise Keynes would not have dealt with the long, long-run problem of 'Economic Possibilities for Our Grandchildren'[3] at a time when he was becoming increasingly preoccupied with the short-run problems of world depression and unemployment. Indeed his prophetic discussions in that 1930 article are such that even so imaginative a book as Professor K. Galbraith's *The Affluent Society* (1958) seems to emerge almost as a hindsight. And few would deny the lively interest which Keynes's pioneering forecast of unprecedented 'economic possibilities' or Professor Galbraith's *The Affluent Society* naturally holds for all developing countries.

The far-reaching impact of Keynes's long-run vision can be further illustrated by reference to some frontier-pushing developments in the postwar period, both theoretical and practical. Keynes's digressive long-run 'breakdown theory' inspired and initiated dynamic analysis in the hands of Sir Roy Harrod, Professor J. R. Hicks and Mrs Joan Robinson in England, just as Professor A. H. Hansen's American counterpart of that theory (i.e. 'the stagnation thesis') led to the development of growth economics by Professor E. D. Domar and

[1] See his *Essays in Persuasion*, pp. 371–3.

[2] Keynes, *Essays in Biography*, p. 141.

[3] See J. A. Schumpeter, 'John Maynard Keynes, 1883–1946', *American Economic Review*, September 1946.

[4] Reproduced in Keynes's *Essays in Persuasion*.

others in the United States. For Keynes warned that if a market economy did not rectify its two 'outstanding faults' (viz., 'its failure to provide full employment and its arbitrary and inequitable distribution of wealth and incomes')[1] through deliberate policy, it would break down sooner or later. That Keynesian warning had the effect of stimulating inquiries into the conditions for 'progressive equilibrium' with full employment but without price inflation.

Without Keynes's *General Theory* and particularly his long-run 'breakdown theory' as a point of departure for dynamic analysis and policy, the experts of the United Nations could not have written their *Measures for the Economic Development of Under-developed Countries* (1951). Nor could another group of UN experts have more recently approved one of them for stating: 'Since capital is the most scarce factor in most underdeveloped economies, the model which suits our purpose best is the Harrod-Domar model.'[2] It seems safe to predict that a balanced blending of Keynes's long-run vision and post-Keynesian growth analysis will continue on a larger and wider scale partly as a consequence of a mounting interest in the underdeveloped economies and partly as a by-product of the competitive efforts of the advanced economies to outstrip each other's growth rate.[3]

It was also Keynes's far-seeing vision of a future 'democracy of nations' the world over as well as of good life at home that led him to play so crucial a role in the postwar establishment of the World Bank and the International Monetary Fund. The underlying Keynesian spirit of multi-national economic co-operation on a 'purely technical and non-political' basis and 'irrespective of the type and principle of government and economic policy existing in the prospective member States'[4] is important for the searchlight it focuses upon the desirability and possibility of international co-existence and co-prosperity in the midst of national diversities, ideological and political. It implies, on the one hand, that the underdeveloped economies desiring multi-national financial assistance need no longer fear such 'political strings' as were historically associated with capital movements and as might still be associated with unilateral lending operations. It implies, on the other hand, that the high-saving economies willing to lend through the multi-national

[1] *General Theory*, p. 372.

[2] See S. Ichimura, 'Appendix to Chapter 11: Macro-Economic Models', in UN, *Programming Techniques for Economic Development With Special Reference to Asia and the Far East*, 1960, p. 81.

[3] Cf. Gov. N. A. Rockefeller, *Accelerated Economic Growth—A Key to the American Future*, 1960.

[4] See *The Keynes Plan* (esp. Preamble).

instrumentalities can now and for ever be spared the traditional stigmas of 'colonialism' and 'imperialism'. The Keynesian spirit of multi-national co-operation, I might add, far transcends any technical defects that may still remain in the existing World Bank and International Monetary Fund.

In addition to the Keynesia scheme of international thinking and policy discussed above, it seems increasingly important to foster those great unifying forces making for a true 'democracy of nations' which are quietly yet powerfully at work below the surface phenomena of disconcerting, exasperating frictions and tensions. I have in mind such subtle peace-makers as art, science, religion, youth movements and sportsmanship—all of which topics are implicit in Keynes's many-sided genius but which can be made a bit more explicit, as in the following delineation.

Art has always been a great unifying force, transcending itself to embrace all humanity and to sweeten life everywhere. For the love of beauty, like love itself, knows no national barriers. Without the creative sensibilities of artists, without the expansiveness and boldness of their imaginations, and without the warmth and depth of their feelings, what a drab, harsh world we would be living in! It is therefore encouraging to witness increasing multi-national and bilateral exchanges of artists to delight all of us and to spread goodwill. Science, like art, is intrinsically cosmopolitan in nature. Thus the seekers of truth have enlightened mankind as a whole just as the lovers of beauty have enriched life in its entirety. Promising, in this respect, are the United Nations Educational, Scientific and Cultural Organization and the International Council of Scientific Union, to mention only the outstanding instances.

Organized religion has persistently been concerned with public morals, social services and world brotherhood. The 1948 formation of the World Council of Churches seems to presage a far-reaching international breakthrough in the field of applied religion. For such a multi-national religious organization importantly supplements other organized efforts to further free and open debates on the great issue of war and peace in this nuclear age. Youth organizations of a cultural nature, instanced by the World Assembly of Youth and America's Peace Corps Programme, seem to be a heartening effort to spread a better understanding among young men and women of divers races and culture. The international idealism and enthusiasm of such youth organizations observably stand in didactic contrast with the cynicism and defeatism of the older generations in some quarters of the world. So sportsmanship, especially of a non-commercial nature, might be regarded as a humble yet salutary adjunct to statesmanship at the international as well as national level. The Olympic Games and such sports meets might accomplish what diplomatic conferences might not—for all we know.

May I close this essay by expressing the hope that my interpretation and extension of Keynes's political economy will stimulate wider discussions on the ways and means of evolving a future community of nations where material abundance is the common lot, where social justice is the household maxim, and democracy and liberty the living realities of life.

APPENDIX I

MR T. BARNA ON BRITISH ECONOMIC GROWTH*

Barna's monograph (prepared for the British National Institute of Economic and Social Research) not only gives insights into the slow yet stable growth of the postwar British economy but also contains much that is instructive for the growth policies of the American economy in general and American industries in particular. On the basis of comparative investigations of two representative groups of British industries (i.e. 'growing' electrical engineering and 'stable' food processing), Barna draws interesting inferences regarding private investment decisions, and also makes suggestive generalizations respecting policy desiderata.

It is instructive that private investment decisions so relevant to Britain's (and other market economies') stable growth have been favourably influenced by her public policy of maintaining 'a high and stable level of employment' and by increased competition (due to removal of wartime controls, anti-monopoly legislation and liberalized imports). Yet Barna candidly admits the continued existence of 'a vicious circle of restricted growth, weak balance of payments and inflation', and also implies the preferability of 'altering the reaction pattern of the economy' over 'detailed intervention' by the government—as the best way to break that vicious circle. For that 'restricted growth' he seems to blame the static and conservative attitudes of British managements, and approvingly quotes Harold Laski's caricature of the British gentleman-merchant: 'The gentleman would rather lose his income than his uniqueness.'

By way of urging more dynamic and progressive management attitudes, Barna makes the typical British understatement: 'The management which resents the purchasing power of the working classes, which resents the increased role of women as consumers and which equally resents technological innovation in production and in distribution, is unlikely to be successful.' Still, the reader may be left wondering whether the British economy will be able to grow faster merely through such a 'managerial revolution' as Barna seems to recommend without at the same time adopting a more vigorous *public* policy for the growth of investment and productivity.

* This is a portion of my book review of T. Barna's *Investment and Growth Policies in British Industrial Firms* (1962) in *The American Economic Review*, September 1962.

APPENDIX II

PROFESSOR HAAVELMO ON ECONOMIC EVOLUTION*

The material of this book, originally used by Professor Haavelmo as a lecture series at the University of Oslo, was prepared for publication as part of the 'economic analysis series' edited by J. Tinbergen and others and offered 'to stimulate the exchange of scientific information and to reinforce international co-operation in the field of economics'. We are also informed that the author received encouragement from T. Koopmans, and had 'interesting discussions' with R. F. Kahn, Joan Robinson and N. Kaldor. The work here given us by this noted Norwegian econometrician is an attempt to provide a theoretical framework for explaining heterogeneous economic developments in space as well as in time, and for guiding 'a programme of economic homogenization', that is, a programme designed to bring up the productive capacity and living standards of less developed economies to the levels prevailing in highly industrialized ones.

We are first introduced to the relevant traditional theories and methodological problems. Haavelmo singles out Adam Smith, Malthus and Marx as the outstanding forerunners of modern macro-dynamic theories of economic development. Adam Smith is credited with spelling out the division of labour and the accumulation of capital as 'the general determinants of economic progress', while Malthus is honoured for laying a 'cornerstone' of secular dynamics. In properly calling attention to the unrealism involved in Malthus's theory of 'economic stagnation'—an unrealism caused by abstracting from the technological substitution effect (between labour and capital), and from a positive marginal propensity to consume out of profit-income—Haavelmo makes no allusion to Keynes's criticism of Malthus's tacit assumption that the interest rate is equal to zero, thus leaving no scope for a 'cheap money policy' of stimulating investment to counteract stagnation possibilities arising from 'oversaving'. As for Marx, Haavelmo considers it plausible to think of his 'materialistic interpretation of history' as 'the foundation of a dynamic theory of economic evolution of the following nature: Economic institutions, as far as they are man-made, and the material results that they produce, are subject to changes, the driving forces of which are themselves outgrowths of the prevailing economic and social system.' In the author's view, Marx's theory, while it suggests the evolutionary process 'in time', is incapable of explaining economic dissimilarities occurring 'in space'.

* This is my review of T. Haavelmo, *A Study in the Theory of Economic Evolution* (1954), in *Social Research*, Spring 1955.

Turning to the modern scene, Haavelmo regards Schumpeter's theory of development as 'an outgrowth of Marxian and Neo-Marxian thinking', and as equally incapable of explaining how 'these forces (such as innovations) could operate with such obviously different results in the various parts of the globe'. One may find the crucial flaw elsewhere, however—that is, in Schumpeter's tendency to treat 'innovations' as if they were the transcendental driving force operative for all times and all societies. The names of Wicksell, Colin Clark, Ragnar Nurkse, Paul Sweezy, Evsey Domar and W. W. Rostow are also mentioned, but there is no mention of Keynes or Harrod, despite the admittedly Keynesian origin of recent 'growth' discussions.

Most of the rest of the book is devoted to the formal elaboration and refinement of the crude yet penetraining insights of classical thinkers—in a way that is operationally significant for scientific control and prediction. No brief review can do full justice to the technical details found in the main chapters, but it is necessary and desirable to indicate the essence of the various mathematical models constructed to illustrate the whys and wherefores of economic dissimilarities.

Haavelmo first takes up the problem of formal dissimilarities in isolated regions, leaving inter-regional evolutionary differences to later analysis. The central or 'explained' variable of his dynamic systems is the volume of production (X), which is considered the most practical index of economic progress, and which is supposed to depend on such 'explanatory' factors as the size of the employable population (N), the amount of capital stock (K) and the level of know-how (S). These latter 'explanatory' variables are in turn described or characterized by historical, technological, institutional and psychological conditions expressed as 'structural parameters'. As such, 'structural parameters' are the basic data of the theory, to be supplemented by additional information in the form of 'initial conditions', such as the initial amount of capital stock $K(t_0)$, for the consideration of output at some later time. Thus far different evolutionary patterns in isolated regions are attributed to differences in 'structural parameters' or 'initial conditions', or both. For instance, one region may progress more rapidly than another possessing similar cultural characteristics (expressed as 'structural parameters') if the former is enabled to produce more by possessing a larger labour force 'to begin with—$N(t_0)$. Or two regions with similar 'initial conditions' may nevertheless exhibit different patterns of development if they differ with respect to the propensities to work, to save, to learn and to procreate (expressed as 'structural parameters' characterizing the input-output relation, the capital-labour relation, and the like).

Two more sources of economic heterogeneity are considered in some detail: 'stochastic' or random shocks and 'trade effects'. The first of these possible sources is taken into account in order to explain irregular developments due to such random elements as 'wars, new technological discoveries the appearance of leading personalities, spiritual revolutions, and the like'. Haavelmo considers it rather fruitless to argue whether random shocks should be regarded as 'exogenous' or 'endogenous' to the theory, though he admits the alternative of interpreting shocks as 'sudden internal explosions in some of the factors actually included in an exact model, e.g. in some parameters that are assumed to be constant in the exact model'. Here he refers to Marx, saying that 'On the basis of a philosophy compatible with "materialistic interpretation of history" many of these things (supposedly externally given shocks) ought perhaps to be regarded as endogenous factors of a theory of evolution.' But Haavelmo satisfies himself by taking random shocks as 'sudden internal explosions'—the saving ratio, for example, deviating from its equilibrium value relative to the investment ratio, to disturb the otherwise smooth path of dynamic growth. It is not realized that this latter method of treating shocks as endogenous (whether in Harrod's or in Marx's sense) not only strengthens the predictability of evolutionary events but also carries with it more practical policy implications. The main point, however, seems to be that economic disparities are due in part to the different ways in which otherwise similar regions absorb and propagate exogenously or endogenously given shocks.

Lastly, Haavelmo suggests that one region may develop more rapidly than another by possessing a more 'advantageous allotment function'; this function relates a region's output to its input, which in turn depends on the populations, capital stocks and educational levels of the whole inter-regional network of which it is a part. This implies that free trade in goods, capital, knowledge and, perhaps, labour has the effect of promoting a long-run process of 'economic homogenization'. No cognizance is taken, however, of the strong possibility that an underemployed region may find it both necessary and desirable to achieve a measure of self-sufficiency and self-protection, even to the neglect of the principle of comparative advantage based on the assumptions of full employment and technological heterogeneity. Nor is there any discussion of the possible repercussions of international price movements and accompanying terms of trade on domestic economic development and living standards. Nor finally is there any suggestion as to how advanced economies might maintain a steady rate of growth in a way that could help underdeveloped economies to achieve a faster rate of progress.

Most readers would probably agree with Professor Haavelmo's basic premise that inter-temporal, inter-regional and inter-racial comparisons are meaningful in terms of *per capita* living standards. Such a premise seems more helpful to a 'programme of economic homogenization' than the teleological assumption that 'backward' areas exist to serve the purposes of 'advanced' areas, or the methaphysical presupposition that uncivilized peoples feel no less 'richer and happier' than civilized ones. Also, Professor Haavelmo's formal endeavours seem to have gone a long way toward fulfilling the hope that 'the further development of analytical economics along the lines of comparative dynamics . . . will aid in the attack upon . . . the majestic problems of economic development', to borrow from Professor Samuelson's *Foundations*. But there still remains to be accomplished, especially in less developed countries, the practical research which Professor Haavelmo's econometric approach suggests.

APPENDIX III

PROFESSOR LEWIS ON ECONOMIC GROWTH*

This wordy volume under review will probably cause mathematical economists as many 'tears' as T. Haavelmo's mathematical *Theory of Evolution* does literary economists. The patient reader, however, will find in Professor Lewis's new book a thorough, mature, well-balanced appraisal of the problems of economic growth in the perspective of historical experience and in the light of modern economic theory. I shall indicate below what seem to me to be the principal merits and demerits of his book. Let us begin with the merits.

This book provides a useful compendium of the complex, interdependent problems of economic development considered as objects of dispassionate analysis and nonpartisan policy—in a more comprehensive manner than do most books on the subject. As such, the book fully lives up to the title of its author: 'Stanley Jevons Professor of *Political Economy*' (in the University of Manchester),[1] for the author admirably combines economic, political, sociological, historical, institutional and ideological materials in his analysis of a very many-sided subject that would tempt less ambitious and industrious writers to be excessively one-sided. The author has, I think, succeeded in accomplishing what he set out to do, to wit: 'to make not a theory, but a map', as he puts it in his Preface.

The novel feature of Lewis's *Theory of Economic Growth* is the unusual emphasis it gives to the role of government in the economic development of underdeveloped countries. This feature stands in sharp contrast with J. A. Schumpeter's *Theory of Economic Development* with its stress on the role of the private 'entrepreneur' (the other members of the famous trio being 'innovation' and 'credit'). Lest the reader should misunderstand the author, I might add that the kind of government intervention he envisages is in the Keynesian tradition of advocating deliberate State action 'as a balancing factor'—not to supplant but to supplement private initiative. He adduces the logical need for public guidance and assistance not only from historical experience (e.g. the UK, Japan and the USSR) but also from the observable dearth of private entrepreneurship in the actual underdeveloped areas of the world. Moreover, on further reading one will discover that the conflict between Lewis and Schumpeter is more apparent than real, for what the former has done is to broaden the traditional

* This is my review of W. Arthur Lewis, *The Theory of Economic Growth* (1955), in *Econometrica*, January 1957.

[1] Later President of the University College of the West Indies, Jamaica.

notions of the 'profit maker' and the 'saver' to include the State. It is by virtue of the above feature that Lewis's growth theory also differs from the purely *laissez-faire* growth models of R. F. Harrod, E. D. Domar and Haavelmo, to mention only the better known.

Turning now to the demerits, I shall mention only two. The most crucial weakness of the volume under review seems to lie in its utter failure to clarify the operationally significant mechanisms whereby measurable variables and quantitative relations most strategically affect the rate of growth of output (*per capita*, that is). Thus the lengthy chapter on capital, for example, seems largely wasted, since it fails to demonstrate how variations in the quantity and quality of capital might influence the rate of growth of output under specified conditions. The policy makers would, in this respect, find a more helpful guide in the operationally more significant Harrod-Domar model, albeit with due regard for the necessary modifications to apply to underdeveloped economies. This failure is all the more regrettable when viewed in the light of the author's promising statement: 'The central problem in the theory of economic growth is to understand the *process* by which a community is converted from being a 5 per cent to a 12 per cent saver' (pp. 225–6; italics mine). Instead of speculating, as does the author, on the possible reasons for internationally different *ex post* capital-output ratios, it would be much more fruitful to show what would happen to the growth rate if the *ex ante* capital-output ratio, based on plausible assumptions about the nature of technological advance, the elasticity of substitution of factors and the rate of interest, was varied, given certain other structural parameters. Otherwise one would never know whether it is a larger or smaller value of the capital-output ratio that is to be desired for the target rate of growth of output.

'Open' economies are considered, but here again there is no demonstration of precisely how various foreign-trade variables affect the rate of growth of those economies. The author discusses the institutional prerequisites of developmental foreign investment, not the theoretical conditions that must be satisfied if foreign investment is to play a quantitatively significant role in the determination of the level of domestic national income or of the rate of growth of domestic output. Nor is there any demonstration of the ways in which the changing terms of trade or the varying price-income elasticities of demand for imports might affect the economic development of 'open' economies. Lewis's book is, therefore, open to the same kind of criticism as J. Viner's *International Trade and Economic Development* had been subjected to.

The second and last weakness to be mentioned is the author's preclusion of income distribution as a determinant of economic growth. Lewis makes the same error of considering the effect of economic growth on income distribution as does Colin Clark in his *The Conditions of Economic Progress* or S. Kuznets in his 'Economic Growth and Income Inequality' (*American Economic Review*, March 1955)—a consideration apropos of an advanced economy which can afford to take the growth of output as given and then proceed with the investigation of its effect on income distribution. But

APPENDIX III

Lewis's book is presumably concerned with the economic growth of underdeveloped countries, where the relevant question to ask is: How does a given change in income inequality affect capital formation and economic development? The author fails to meet the classical challenge that inequality is a *sine qua non* of economic progress. His implied institutional argument that government saving is capable of compensating for any deficiency of voluntary saving that income equalization might entail seems to be less than cogent. It can be shown that, given the significantly different marginal productivities of agricultural and industrial capital, a redistribution of real capital (e.g. from agriculture to industry) could increase the productivity of capital for the economy as a whole, as evidenced by the phenomenal industrialization of Japan (cf., M. Shinohara, 'Economic Progress and Price Structure', *Economic Review*, Hitotsubashi University, July 1954). It can also be shown that an increase in income inequality (a decrease in the ratio of wages to a given national income) does not necessarily lead to greater aggregate savings, contrary to the classical reasoning. For if greater income disparities had the effect of increasing both wage-earners' and profit-takers' desire to consume more for reasons of 'emulation' and 'prestige' respectively, the marginal propensities to save of both groups could decrease to offset any increasing effect that greater inequality might have on total savings when the marginal propensity to save out of profit-income exceeds that out of wage-income. Thus to agree, tacitly or otherwise, with the classical proposition that 'the abstinence of the rich' is necessary for greater saving is to ignore the sociological phenomena of 'emulation' and 'prestige' in estimating the long-run impact of income redistribution on consumer habits—to which phenomena J. S. Duesenberry has referred as the 'demonstration effect' which R. Nurkse has in turn applied to capital-poor economies exposed to the necessity of keeping up with the international Joneses (cf., Nurkse, *Problems of Capital Formation in Underdeveloped Countries*).

In sum, the present volume is strong on the whys of economic growth and weak on the hows of it. The reader must decide for himself on which side the balance is tipped.

APPENDIX IV

SIR ROY HARROD ON THE DOLLAR IN WORLD AFFAIRS*

Mr Harrod tells us that the book under review is based on his George Watson lectures on American history, literature and institutions delivered at Oxford, and so he prepares us for a broader appraisal of the dollar than if he were addressing himself to monetary experts alone. The descriptive material of the first two lectures on 'Evolution of the Dollar' and 'The Federal Reserve System' is obviously designed to provide a historical perspective for the more analytical and substantive material of the subsequent lectures on 'Towards International Co-operation' and 'The Dollar Gap'. It is in the last lecture that Mr Harrod spells out most clearly what he set himself to do, i.e. to state his view of 'the causes of what we have come to know recently as the "dollar problem"'. In fact he does much more than that, because he offers operationally significant policy suggestions as well.

Mr Harrod makes a useful distinction between the dollar gap of a transitory nature and the dollar gap of a persistent nature. He attributes the former type to 'overspending and inflationary pressures in the non-dollar countries' roughly from 1946 to 1951. There is an implied criticism of those who talk as if the dollar gap would never exist, much less persist, if only the non-dollar countries live within their means, that is, do not aspire to keep up with the Joneses of the dollar-countries. At any rate Mr Harrod warns that 'a country may have no internal inflation and yet not achieve an external balance'. Thus he makes clear that it is not a simple matter of 'disinflating' the propensities to invest, to consume, and to import in the non-dollar countries, including the war-devastated ones, before there can be general currency convertibility and multilateral trade.

Mr Harrod does not systematically put down the causes of the chronic dollar shortage (the second type), but he discusses some of them and implies others in connection with policy considerations. The following causes are discernible in his discussions: (*a*) the 'great shifts in the pattern of world trade' caused by the war, necessitating 'permanent structural readjustments' which cannot be made during the 'transition period' in the usual sense of this latter expression; (*b*) a determination throughout the non-dollar world not to cure an external deficit by the classical medicine, that is, by submitting to 'an unlimited amount of unemployment' at home, thus ruling out the familiar deflationary (as distinguished from 'dis-inflationary') method of lowering domestic wages, prices (including export

* This is my review of R. F. Harrod, *The Dollar: the History and Position of the Dollar in World Affairs* (1954), in *Econometrica*, April 1955.

prices) and incomes until the consequential increase in exports and decrease in imports restore equilibrium in the balance of payments; (*c*) 'the fixity of the dollar price of gold' despite the doubled price level of goods, which fixity tends to depress gold production in the non-dollar countries, to reduce international liquidity (i.e. gold as the principal medium of monetary reserve against external accounts), and to prevent otherwise possible financial settlements with the dollar areas; (*d*) the continued 'protectionism' of the United States despite her position as the world's greatest creditor; and (*e*) the technical weaknesses of the International Monetary Fund. Some comment on this formidable list of long-term causes is in order.

In order to meet the 'shifts in the pattern of world trade' it is necessary, according to Mr Harrod, to make such 'structural readjustments' in the non-dollar countries' production and exportation as to 'win large new markets abroad', especially in the Western Hemisphere (e.g. Canada and Latin American markets), where 'there is a supply of new US dollars available for capture'. Apart from the technical difficulty of readjusting European industrial structures (including export industries) to suit the tastes and needs of the dollar areas on the other side of the Atlantic, Mr Harrod seems to preclude altogether the possibility of capturing dollars and gold in East European and Far Eastern markets. It is interesting, by contrast, that Mrs Joan Robinson, who recently accompanied a British trade mission to Mainland China, does not preclude such a possibility. Everyone today would agree with Mr Harrod's emphasis that 'if the choice were between massive unemployment and the imposition of discriminatory restrictions, the latter would be preferred'. Yet when Mr Harrod rejects, as we all should, discriminatory restrictions on dollar imports as a permanent feature in favour of 'tentative, provisional, reversible, small, stage-by-stage reductions' in the external value of deficit countries' currencies presumably through national Exchange Equalization Accounts, instead of a 'once-over movement in the parity' now sanctioned by the International Monetary Fund, one wonders whether Mr Harrod may have gone too far in the direction of 'free' exchange markets. Moreover, there is an insufficient consideration of the *income* elasticity of demand for imports in Mr Harrod's criticism of the price elasticity as a reliable criterion of currency devaluation. Such a consideration is important when one contemplates, as does Mr Harrod, expanded trade with under-developed dollar areas (including Latin America which is one of his targets) whose demand for imports is believed to be more elastic with respect to domestic income than with respect to foreign price.

Now comes Mr Harrod's real prize, that is, the rigidity of the dollar price of gold which is in his view 'the biggest cause' of the dollar problem. The key to this point of view is found in his earlier remark (Lecture 2, p. 68) that 'the increase in the dollar price raised world liquidity and enabled nations striving to recover to pursue a more liberal policy than they could otherwise have done'—a remark made in his retrospective comment on the 1933 devaluation of the dollar. Mr Harrod's thought seems to be that if the United States agrees to raise the dollar price of gold to compensate for the postwar fall in the purchasing power of gold, non-dollar countries will be stimulated to produce and acquire more new gold for monetary use and so to liberalize their present trade restrictions on dollar goods. He is, of course, quite aware of American objections to the idea of changing the dollar price of gold, but he does not consider them to be as important as the more fundamental objections to the continuation of currency inconvertibility, bilateral trade and other deterrents to the restoration of multilateral trade. I have two reservations, however. One of them is that the *distribution* of gold, old or new, as a medium of monetary reserve among non-dollar countries may be more crucial than the aggregate quantity of gold that is supposed to govern 'world liquidity'. Some non-dollar countries which do not produce much gold themselves or cannot readily acquire gold by achieving export surpluses elsewhere would not be able to take full advantage of the higher price of gold. Moreover, underdeveloped non-dollar countries might well receive little or no developmental capital from the US if the latter settled its current credits not by lending long-term capital, but by allowing debtor countries to pay higher-valued gold—unless the resources of the World Bank can be considered adequate for the purpose. Apart from these reservations, I think that Mr Harrod's bold proposal merits serious consideration.

Little needs to be said about the 'protectionism' of the US as an impediment to general currency convertibility and multilateralism inasmuch as American officialdom seems determined to remove it, albeit slowly, if we judge by the liberal recommendations of the Douglas Report (July 14, 1953) and the Randall Commission. As for the technical weaknesses of the International Monetary Fund, Mr Harrod rightly criticizes the arbitrary aspect of the otherwise important 'scarce currency clause' which would, if the situation warranted it, permit deficit countries to discriminate against surplus countries whose currencies are declared 'scarce' relative to world demand. He goes further and recommends the revamping of the Fund along the original lines of *The Keynes Plan*, with a view to making it a truly central bank or an International Federal Reserve System capable of using monetary policy for both countercyclical and balance-of-payments purposes.

Such, in brief, are Mr Harrod's diagnosis of and cures for the dollar problem. Whether one agrees or disagrees with his diagnosis and cures, one must read Mr Harrod's book with an open mind just as he has written it with all the technical skills, urbanities and subtleties at his command. His book is a very welcome contribution to the great debate in which Dr T. Balogh, Professor J. E. Meade, Professor G. Haberler, Professor C. P. Kindleberger and others have already participated.[1]

[1] Sir Roy Harrod's plea for a revamping of the International Monetary Fund along the lines of *The Keynes Plan* anticipated the appearance of the so-called 'Triffin Plan', though the latter was prompted by the more recent problem of 'the dollar crisis'. See, in this latter connection, R. Triffin, *Gold and the Dollar Crisis* (1960); K. V. Gowda, 'Keynes-Triffin Plans and International Liquidity', *Kautilya*, January 1962; and my 'Cost Disinflation and Export Expansion', *Kyklos*, Vol. XIV, 1961.

INDEX

INDEX

GEORGE ALLEN & UNWIN LTD
London: 40 Museum Street, W.C.1

Auckland: 24 Wyndham Street
Bombay: 15 Graham Road, Ballard Estate, Bombay 1
Buenos Aires: Escritorio 454–459, Florida 165
Calcutta: 17 Chittaranjan Avenue, Calcutta 13
Cape Town: 109 Long Street
Hong Kong: F1/12 Mirador Mansions, Kowloon
Ibadan: P.O. Box 62
Karachi: Karachi Chambers, McLeod Road
Madras: Mohan Mansions, 38c Mount Road, Madras 6
Mexico: Villalongin 32–10, Piso, Mexico 5, D.F.
Nairobi: P.O. Box 4536
New Delhi: 13–14 Asaf Ali Road, New Delhi 1
São Paulo: Avenida 9 de Julho 1138-Ap. 51
Singapore: 36c Prinsep Street, Singapore 7
Sydney, N.S.W.: Bradbury House, 55 York Street
Tokyo: 3 Kanda-Ogawamachi, 3-Chome, Chiyoda-ku
Toronto: 91 Wellington Street West, Toronto 1

OM PRAKASH

THEORY AND WORKING OF STATE CORPORATIONS

Dr Prakash has written an incisive work on a subject of great and growing interest to India and to other countries planning a rapid development. He studies each of the Indian State Corporations, including Public Corporations and the 'Government Companies'.

The system of State Corporations is set in its historical background, their characteristics are examined in theory, and those in India compared to those elsewhere. With acute and independent judgment Dr Prakash examines the merits and defects of each Corporation and of each class of Corporation in practice, from which he is able to make a series of important practical recommendations.

Demy 8vo. 30s. net

FREDERIC **L. PRYOR**

THE COMMUNIST **FOREIGN** TRADE SYSTEM

Here is a broad fascinating study of the 'other' Common Market. Dr Pryor surveys the extent of economic integration between the European communist nations. He analyses the new communist foreign trade institutions and pays particular attention to the problems of economic planning and decision making. He makes it possible for the reader to estimate the extent to which the communist nations are adapting themselves to a more rational trading system. The changing pattern of economic exploitation is revealed by a penetrating scrutiny of the foreign trade prices of these nations and the author also thoroughly examines the economic motives behind the geographical pattern of trade.

This analysis is the result of two years of extensive research. Dr Pryor gathered his materials not only from all the published foreign trade literature of the communist countries, but also from a great many personal interviews with communist foreign trade officials and economists in East Berlin—the cost of these attempts at a clear and objective understanding of the communist foreign trade system being six months' imprisonment, without formal charge or trial, in East Germany.

Demy 8vo. 40s. net

www.ingramcontent.com/pod-product-compliance
Lightning Source LLC
LaVergne TN
LVHW021112300926
849160LV00009B/703

* 9 7 8 0 4 1 5 6 0 7 8 5 8 *